NO CHILD LEFT BEHIND

Past, Present, and Future

William Hayes

ROWMAN & LITTLEFIELD EDUCATION
Lanham • New York • Toronto • Plymouth, UK

Published in the United States of America
by Rowman & Littlefield Education
A Division of Rowman & Littlefield Publishers, Inc.
A wholly owned subsidary of The Rowman & Littlefield Publishing Group, Inc.
4501 Forbes Boulevard, Suite 200, Lanham, Maryland 20706
www.rowmaneducation.com

Estover Road
Plymouth PL6 7PY
United Kingdom

British Library Cataloguing in Publication Information Available

Library of Congress Cataloging-in-Publication Data

Hayes, William, 1938–
 No Child Left Behind : past, present, and future / William Hayes.
  p. cm.
 ISBN-13: 978-1-57886-835-3 (cloth : alk. paper)
 ISBN-10: 1-57886-835-1 (cloth : alk. paper)
 eISBN-10: 1-57886-897-1
 eISBN-13: 978-1-57886-897-1
 1. United States. No Child Left Behind Act of 2001. 2. Educational
accountability—United States. 3. Education—Standards—United States.
4. Educational tests and measurements—United States. I. Title.
 LB2806.22.H395 2008
 379.1'580973—dc22   2008010890

With this, the completion of my twelfth book for Rowman & Littlefield, I wish to offer my sincere gratitude to my wife Nancy. She has proofread, made suggestions, and helped with the indexes of all of the books. Most of all, I will be forever grateful for her support and patience as I pursue these projects.

CONTENTS

FOREWORD

Adam Urbanski

It was January 2002 and the Elementary and Secondary Education Act had just been reauthorized. There was much anticipation and a buzz about it in the air. It had a catchy and lofty title, "No Child Left Behind" (NCLB), and bipartisan support. It featured positive expressions of support from respected education and social advocates such as Marian Wright Edelman and Linda Darling-Hammond.

This was the central topic of conversation at the winter 2002 meeting of the executive council of the American Federation of Teachers. By then, NCLB had already earned the tongue-in-cheek definition of a "classic"—a book that everyone has heard of but virtually nobody has read. My colleagues, most of them longtime teacher-union leaders, were tripping over themselves heaping praise on this "landmark legislation."

I was astounded. Had the Bush administration actually persuaded everyone that this ill-advised piece of legislation represented the answer to our education problems? And why was the reception here so unlike what I heard teachers say? I felt a moral obligation to not remain silent on the issue.

"If this law were to be fully implemented it would result in the dismantling of public school in America—beginning with urban districts,"

I asserted. But nobody else weighed in. Instead, I was admonished that "this is exactly the kind of alarmism and negativism that we do not need."

So here we are, six years later. Most teachers continue to oppose NCLB, as does most of the public. Even those who supported it in the past are now in favor of "fixing" it. But, amazingly, even the staunch opponents of NCLB are still pressing for fully funding all its provisions—even those they consider destructive. Wouldn't it make more sense to cut off funding for a law that is considered destructive?

Democrats and Republicans in Congress are increasingly reluctant to reauthorize NCLB. By now, the question is not just how long it'll be delayed, but rather whether it'll be reauthorized at all. Democratic presidential candidate Hillary Clinton told New York City's United Federation of Teachers that NCLB should be "scrapped."

NCLB attaches high stakes to standardized tests, narrows the curriculum, labels schools unfairly, siphons away much-needed funds from impoverished districts and schools, and allows privateers to prey on public-school children. More and more teachers tell me, "I love to teach, but hate my job." They feel increasingly concerned about the destructive impact of NCLB on the teaching and learning environment. And the growing frustration has turned to anger.

Yet, the federal government is not going to lessen its influence on public education. Historically, its influence has been considerably weaker than the influence of state and local government. But as our society becomes more diverse and equity more valued, the role of the federal government is likely to only increase.

This is why *No Child Left Behind: Past, Present, and Future* is such important reading. The author is eminently qualified to take on the task because of his long and accomplished career as a teacher, administrator, and college professor. He examines the history of the law, comments on its current status, and projects its likely future, all from both academic and pragmatic perspectives. This represents an invaluable context for those who want to better understand the law—and an even more critical context for those who want to amend or change it.

The best thing that could be said about NCLB is that there was good intent, especially when it comes to disaggregating data for the purpose of ensuring the success of *all* categories of students. But the worst things about the NCLB are the logistics and implementation guidelines, which are unworkable at best and hurtful in many ways. Good intentions do not mitigate the actual damage caused. When it comes to accountability, especially, it is the precisely the details that are key. And when it comes to NCLB, the cure seems worse than the disease.

Proponents and foes of NCLB alike want better education for all students. The prospects for making progress toward that goal are enhanced if the debate is both contextualized and depolarized. William Hayes's excellent book makes an important contribution toward that end.

Adam Urbanski, PhD
President, Rochester (NY) Teachers Association
Vice President, American Federation of Teachers

ACKNOWLEDGMENTS

There are two very special people who assisted in the preparation of this book. For the first three chapters, my student assistant was junior Daisy Algarin. She typed these chapters and helped with the initial research. When Daisy was no longer able to continue, I was very fortunate to have the able assistance of graduate student Melodee Buchanan for the remainder of the project. Melodee became a true partner as she became involved in every phase of the work. She was especially talented at proofreading and the index. Without the contributions of these two fine young women, this book would not have been possible.

INTRODUCTION

During the approximately six years since its implementation, the federal legislation known as No Child Left Behind has had a major effect on public education in the United States. Passed with bipartisan support by a Republican Congress and signed by an enthusiastic President Bush on January 2, 2002, the hundreds of pages of the law have touched every public-school classroom in our country. The mandates included have affected the content and methods used by teachers as well as the training they have received prior to entering the profession. Most importantly, the law has made a difference in the lives of children and families as additional pressures for accountability have been placed on their schools.

This book first considers the reasons for the passage of the legislation, as well as its goals. Because of the controversies surrounding the law, there will be an extensive discussion of the concerns of its critics. As a result of pressures from many sources, the initial regulations established to guide the implementation have been revised and the implications of these changes will be examined in detail.

In the second part of the book, there is an in-depth analysis of the academic and nonacademic results of the legislation. This section focuses specifically on test scores in language arts and math, along with the possible effects of the law on other areas of the curriculum. The charge that teachers are now merely "teaching to the test" will also be considered. In addition, there is discussion of the progress that has been achieved in meeting other objectives of the law. This section includes an analysis of such mandates as the requirement that schools employ only highly competent teachers, as well as the goal of creating safer schools. Additional attention is given to the choice options included in the legislation.

The final section of the book deals with an overview of the current status of the legislation. Attention is given to the views of the major political parties, the effect of the 2008 elections, and the positions being taken by the various groups involved in education. Using these data, the book ends with some tentative predictions regarding the fate of the reform initiative that has occurred as a result of the passage of the law.

The subject of this book should be of interest to every American. There is no question that the future of our nation will always be affected by the quality of our public schools. More than any recent event, the passage of the No Child Left Behind law has significantly affected the way we are educating our children. My hope is that this book will help readers to better understand what is really happening in our schools.

I

THE PAST

①

HISTORICAL BACKGROUND

During the first 250 years of our nation's history, schools in the United States were either the responsibility of local communities or were sponsored by various religious denominations. Neither the federal nor the state government had any involvement in the field of education. It is true that the Congress under the Articles of Confederation did recognize the importance of establishing schools. The Land Ordinance of 1785, along with the 1787 Northwest Ordinance, outlined the settlement policy for the territory bordering the Great Lakes. Townships in this area were to be divided into thirty-six sectors. It was mandated that one sector in each township should be "set aside for the support of public education."[1]

The same year as the passage of the Northwest Ordinance, a meeting was held in Philadelphia to draft a new constitution. The product of these deliberations established a much stronger federal government than the Articles of Confederation had, but nowhere in the document is there a mention of education or schools as a power to be exercised by the new central government. In 1791, following the ratification of the constitution, the first ten amendments, known as the Bill of Rights, were passed by the Congress and ratified by the necessary number of states. The tenth of these amendments seemed aimed at restricting federal incursion into areas such as education. It states that "the powers not delegated to the United States by the Constitution nor prohibited by it to the States, are reserved to the States respectively, or to the people."[2]

The public-school system as we know it today did not begin to emerge on a significant scale until midway through the nineteenth century. Horace Mann, an educational leader from Massachusetts, has been given a great deal of the credit for the establishment of a free, publicly supported school system in the United States. Labeled by many historians as the "father of the common schools" or even the "father of the public schools," Mann spent much of his adult life advocating for the cause of public education, which he believed was the "greatest discovery ever made by man."[3] Among his contributions was his success in convincing the Massachusetts Legislature to contribute financially to both the support of public schools and the training of teachers. Similar movements began slowly in every state, and we have now reached the point where state governments supply the largest portion of financial support to the public schools.[4]

As the states assumed more control in the nineteenth and early twentieth centuries, there was little consideration given to a federal role in the field of education. Still, Horace Mann, upon giving up his position as the secretary of the Board of Education in Massachusetts, did at least consider the possibility of federal involvement. Later, as a member of the United States House of Representatives, he introduced legislation that would have created a Department of Education in Washington.[5] Needless to say, the nation would not create such a federal agency for over a century.

There have been several milestones in the story of federal involvement in education in the twentieth century. The first major event was instigated neither by Congress nor the president. In 1954, with the decision in the case of *Brown v. the Board of Education of Topeka, Kansas*, a unanimous Supreme Court struck down the reigning legal doctrine established by the 1896 case of *Plessy v. Ferguson*. In this earlier decision, the court had ruled that public facilities such as schools that were separated by race were legal as long as they were equal. The so-called "separate but equal" doctrine was declared inherently unequal in the *Brown* decision. This case began a prolonged process that saw the federal government enforcing school racial integration.

The following decade of the 1960s saw President Lyndon Johnson initiating a major legislative program to end poverty in our country. In assessing ways to assist poor people, the president and the Congress became convinced of the failure of schools to prepare poor children to succeed in our society. Thus the "war on poverty" featured several major initiatives in the field of education. Of these, the most important was the Elementary Secondary Education Act, passed in 1965. It was the reauthorized version of this legislation that was titled No Child Left Behind.

The most significant part of the law is contained in the section known as Title I, which provided a large new financial aid package for local schools. Title I was designed specifically to improve the reading and math skills of poor children. Under it, a local school district received funds based on the number of poor children enrolled.

An additional law that had a major effect on the field of education was passed during the same time period. Known as the Head Start Program, it provided money and guidelines that allowed local communities to create preschool programs for poor children.

In 1968, Congress focused on another group of children when it passed the Bilingual Education Act. This law attempted to require school districts to provide appropriate programs for children in their schools who had inadequate skills in using the English language.[6]

Even under the Republican administration of Richard Nixon, the federal government moved further into the field of public education. In order to ensure that female students were not discriminated against in any way, Congress passed Title IX of the Education Amendments in 1972.

A major new regulation that has had very significant effect on public schools was passed in 1975. Public Law 94-142, or the Individuals with Disabilities Education Act, mandated that schools provide a free and appropriate education to students identified as having disabilities. The law required that schools establish a whole new system to identify and properly educate those children who were classified as disabled. Although this and several other of the federal education laws did provide some financial aid, school districts as well as the state governments often had to raise additional funds to implement the laws.

As the country entered the 1980s, there were an increasing number of critics calling for federal intervention in what was perceived by many as a failing system of education in our country. Among those seeking changes were business leaders who believed that our schools were not adequately preparing students for an increasingly competitive world economy. For them, the failures in education were a major factor in causing the economic problems facing the nation. There was no question that the economy was in trouble. When Ronald Reagan assumed the presidency in 1981, the national unemployment rate was 10.7 percent. There were an increasing number of bankruptcies and farm foreclosures. While the economy was sluggish, the nation was facing an inflation rate of 12.5 percent. In seeking to limit increases in the cost of living, the Federal Reserve System had raised the prime interest rate to over 21 percent. A unique economic situation in our history, the trend was labeled by economists and political leaders as "stagflation."[7]

It was not only the pressures of the poor economy that stimulated federal action in the field of education. Critics throughout the United States were becoming increasingly unhappy with the public schools. They were especially unhappy with the performance of our high schools. These critics believed the schools had abandoned the basic academic skills and there was a need to go "back to basics." During this period, one prominent educational author, E. D. Hirsch, wrote:

> The common knowledge characteristically shared by those at the top of the socioeconomic ladder in the United States should be readily available to all citizens because people who lack it suffer serious handicaps. This "core knowledge" is needed for productive communication and in establishing fundamental equality as citizens. That is the content of basic education and should be the primary focus of schooling.[8]

In 1981, despite a lack of support by key Republican leaders, newly appointed Secretary of Education Terrel Bell decided to establish a representative task force to recommend ways to improve our nation's schools. After a year of hearings and gathering information, the group's final product was introduced to the nation by President Reagan. Titled *A Nation at Risk*, the report captured the attention of the media as well as the leaders of state government. The most widely quoted portion of the document pictured an educational system facing a crisis. The introduction included this much-quoted paragraph:

> Our Nation is at risk. Our once unchallenged prominence in commerce, industry, science, and technological innovation is being overtaken by competitors throughout the world. . . . If an unfriendly foreign power had attempted to impose on America the mediocre educational performance that exists today, we might well have viewed it as an act of war. As it stands, we have allowed this to happen to ourselves. We have even squandered the gains in student achievement made in the wake of the Sputnik challenge. Moreover, we have dismantled essential support systems, which helped make those gains possible. We have, in effect, been committing an act of unthinking, unilateral educational disarmament.[9]

Among the findings of the group were the following:

- International comparisons of student achievement, completed a decade ago, reveal that on nineteen academic tests American students were never first or second and, in comparison with other industrialized nations, were last seven times.
- Some 23 million American adults are functionally illiterate by the simplest tests of everyday reading, writing, and comprehension.
- About 13 percent of all seventeen-year-olds in the United States can be considered functionally illiterate.
- Average achievement of high school students on most standardized tests is now lower than twenty-six years ago when Sputnik was launched.
- The College Board's Scholastic Aptitude Tests (SAT) demonstrate virtually unbroken decline from 1963 to 1980. Average verbal scores fell over fifty points, and average mathematics scores dropped nearly forty points.
- There was a steady decline in science achievement scores of U.S. seventeen-year-olds as measured by national assessments of science in 1969, 1973, and 1977.
- Average tested achievement of students graduating from college is also lower.

- Business and military leaders complain that they are required to spend millions of dollars on costly remedial education and training programs in such basic skills as reading, writing, spelling, and computation. The Department of the Navy, for example, reported to the Commission that one-quarter of its recent recruits cannot read at the ninth grade level, the minimum needed simply to understand written safety instructions.[10]

After identifying the problems, the report goes on to make specific recommendations for improving schools. Many of these recommendations were the seeds for the educational reform movement that occurred in the 1980s and 1990s. More importantly, they provided much of the rationale for the No Child Left Behind legislation. Included were such ideas as the need for states to develop curriculum standards. This meant that for every subject being taught, there should be a careful articulation of what students should know and be able to do in that academic discipline. To ensure that children were truly learning, the report called for a testing program to measure student achievement. Test scores were to be made public and schools held accountable. There were also recommendations on how best to improve the teaching profession.

The language included foreshadowed many of the specific mandates contained in No Child Left Behind. While earlier national legislation highlighted specific groups of children, the objectives sought by the *Nation at Risk* recommendations were aimed not at any single group, but rather at every child. The authors wrote that "all, regardless of race or class or economic status, are entitled to a fair chance and to the tools for developing their individual powers of mind and spirit to the utmost."[11] Although there were numerous other studies and reports during the 1980s, historian Diane Ravitch has written:

> A *Nation at Risk* was a landmark of education reform literature. Countless previous reports by prestigious national commissions had been ignored by the national press and the general public. A *Nation at Risk* was different. Written in stirring language that the general public could understand, the report warned that schools had not kept pace with the changes in society and the economy and that the nation would suffer if education were not dramatically improved for all children. It also as-

serted that lax academic standards were correlated with lax behavior standards and that neither should be ignored. *A Nation at Risk* was a call to action.[12]

The very positive public reaction to the report caused President Reagan to use educational reform as a talking point during his election campaign in 1984. During his second term, a number of initiatives were carried out at the state level. They included such things as increased graduation requirements, the development of new testing and accountability procedures, and attempts to improve the teaching profession.[13] President Reagan's successor, George H. W. Bush, was even more interested in the field of education. It was his goal to be called the "Education President," and he moved the process forward by calling together all of the governors to create a list of educational objectives for the nation. Labeled *Goals 2000*, these ambitious objectives were to provide an agenda that was to be completed by the end of the century. One of the leaders in this effort was the young Arkansas governor, Bill Clinton.

Between 1989 and 1992, most of the states developed curriculum standards, high-stakes tests, and procedures attempting to hold schools accountable for student learning. When Bill Clinton assumed the presidency in 1993, he too was committed to the idea of using the federal government to improve schools. He was willing to go much further than the previous Republican administration as he supported efforts to develop national curriculums in several subject areas. Although never adopted as a national curriculum, the work of the standards committee on mathematics he convened has been used as a guide by many of the states. On the other hand, the effort to produce a national curriculum in social studies ended in fierce controversy.

The other most significant activity by the national government in the field of education during the Clinton years was the passage, in 1994, of the Improving American Schools Act. Like No Child Left Behind, this law came as a result of the debate over reauthorizing the Elementary Secondary Education Act. The wording of the new law expanded the goals from improving the education of disadvantaged children to seeking to make a positive difference for all children.[14] When George W. Bush took office in 2001, forty-eight states, along with the District of Columbia and Puerto Rico, had received approval by the federal government of their content standards development process, and twenty-four states had completed their performance standards.[15] Thus some of the work that would be required by No Child Left Behind had already begun.

One of the explanations for the passage of No Child Left Behind in 2001 is that it was merely the next step in the continuing trend of federal government involvement in the field of education. The historic Republican view that public schools should be a responsibility of state and local government had been weakening. This was true despite the fact that a number of conservative members of the party continued to oppose any new federal legislation in the area. The Democratic party and less conservative Republicans were ready for additional federal intervention. The fact that test scores of American students continued to lag behind scores of children in other developed countries led a large majority in both houses to consider a stronger role by the federal government. The fact that for almost a half century we had been moving in this direction made the dramatic changes mandated in No Child Left Behind much less controversial.

It is certainly true that the historical trend toward increased federal involvement in education during the second half of the twentieth century was a major factor that made passage of the law possible. The increased political importance of this issue is demonstrated in a public poll that ranks the most important problems facing the nation during presidential election years. In the 1980 election, education was rated twenty-third out of forty-one issues. By 2000, education was named the most important problem facing the nation.[16] This, along with the continuing public perception that our schools should be doing better, certainly helped to create a favorable climate for educational reform. There was also the traditional desire of liberals to help the poor and disadvantaged. For Democrats, this almost always was accomplished by providing additional financial aid to schools. Powerful Democrats, such as Senator Ted Kennedy, were ready to negotiate with their Republican colleagues and the new president if it could result in providing more federal money to help educate poor and minority children. It should be pointed out that despite all of the federal education initiatives, including No Child Left Behind, the federal contribution for financing schools has never exceeded 8 percent of the money spent on them.

A second factor that helped to make passage of the law possible was the election of George W. Bush as president. As part of his campaign, he highlighted his accomplishments in the field of education as governor of Texas. He talked frequently about how his leadership had helped to bring about an improvement of test scores in his state labeled the "Texas Miracle." Bush was able to push his plans despite the fact that his party was still divided over the role of the federal government in education. As the party's presidential candidate, he had to lobby hard to ensure that the party platform in 2000 did not contain the same call for the abolition of the Department of Education that had been included in the platform of the party during the two previous presidential elections. On campaign stops, Bush talked about the testing programs created in Texas. He especially emphasized the gains made by black and Latino students.[17]

Some who examined the alleged successes of the Texas program were less than impressed. In a report completed by the Center for the Study of Testing at Boston College, the authors noted that the drop-out rate increased after the implementation of the program in Texas. This was especially true with minority students. It was suggested that schools were "pushing large numbers of kids out" in order to raise the average scores. "In other words, if the poorest students drop out, then you can expect that scores will improve."[18] A Harvard researcher who analyzed the Texas tests concluded that the standards on the reading test had been lowered each year between 1995 and 1998. It has also been noted that as governor, Bush opposed the decision of the Texas Supreme Court that required that state aid be reduced for the richer districts and increased for poorer districts. Many believe that equal financial resources for all schools is an important factor in equalizing educational opportunities for all children, but the governor could not support this so-called "Robin Hood principle."[19]

Even if Governor Bush's improved test scores might be controversial, there is no question that he did "forcefully move" the reforms begun by his predecessor, Ann Richards, through the Texas Legislature. His record helped him in his campaign against Al Gore, who "never

really found his voice on education." As part of the Republican platform, candidate Bush supported the following:

- Private school vouchers
- Phonics-based reading programs
- Character education
- Abstinence-only sex education

The party also endorsed state curriculum standards and high-stakes
testing.[20]

Along with the historical momentum and the leadership of President Bush, there is one other explanation that has been offered for the
passage of No Child Left Behind. There have been those who saw the
law as a secret conspiracy by conservatives to destroy the public-
school system as we know it. These critics suggest that conservatives
expect the public schools to fail and thus the nation will then be ready
to turn to a free-enterprise voucher system that would allow private
religious schools as well as for-profit schools to successfully compete
with the failing public schools.[21] In the words of one of the law's most
outspoken critics, Alfie Kohn, the "idea of reform turns out to entail
some sort of privatization, such that education is gradually transferred
to the marketplace. There, the bottom line is not what benefits children but what produces profit."[22]

Whether any of the supporters of the law were actually plotting to
destroy the public schools or not, there remains a strong conviction
among conservatives that school choice is the answer to our nation's
educational woes. There are many who believe that a voucher system
that allows families to receive government funds to pay for their children's attendance at either private or public schools would greatly improve education. They believe it would do so by introducing free competition into a market where the public schools currently have a
significant advantage. Supporters of such a system include President
Bush and a number of important leaders in the Republican party.

In the extended discussions leading up to the passage of No Child
Left Behind, the Bush administration fought hard for the inclusion of
a national voucher program. In the end, the Republicans settled for
much less dramatic choice options. The Democrats also had to make

a number of compromises during the debates. Some of them supported the development of national curriculum standards and tests. For them, allowing each state to determine what was to be taught and how it was to be tested would result in uneven standards and the inability to compare results among the states. Conservatives insisted that the states keep the power to develop standards as well as tests.

In return for allowing the states the autonomy to develop their own programs, the Democrats extracted a significant increase in funding for schools and were able to exclude a national voucher system. Along with the standards and testing provisions, the final bill contained numerous miscellaneous provisions that deal with a wide variety of legislative concerns. There are provisions to ensure teacher quality, school safety, and drug education; a section dealing with school prayer; a granting of the right to visit high schools to military recruiters; and even a clause that ensures that the Boy Scouts of America have access to school buildings. Undoubtedly, the inclusion of the favorite causes of various legislators helped to gain wide-scale support for the law. The final product, though, was described by a Hoover Institution publication as being "at once numbingly detailed and comfortably vague." The final vote in the Senate was 87 in favor and only 10 opposed. In the House of Representatives, 381 members voted for the bill, with only 41 registering a negative vote.

Thus it was with significant bipartisan support that President Bush signed the No Child Left Behind Act in January 2002. There was a great deal of optimism in Washington that this legislation could make a positive difference in our nation's schools.

Prior to attempting to analyze the effect of No Child Left Behind, it would seem helpful to highlight significant sections of the law. This review will be the subject of the next chapter.

NOTES

1. Ruth Wood Gavian and William A. Hamm, *United States History* (Lexington, Mass.: D.C. Heath, 1960), 135.

2. George Brown Tindall, *America, A Narrative History* (New York: W.W. Norton, 1984), 23.

3. Mary Peabody Mann, *The Life and Works of Horace Mann* (Boston: Lee and Shephard Publishers, 1891), 142.

4. David Miller Sadker, Myra Pollack Sadker, and Karen R. Zittleman, *Teachers, Schools, and Society* (Boston: McGraw-Hill, 2008), 354.

5. Mann, *Horace Mann*, 259.

6. Sadker, Sadker, and Zittleman, *Teachers, Schools, and Society*, 75.

7. Time-Life Books, *Pride and Prosperity: The 80s* (Alexandria, Va.: Time-Life Books, 1999), 24–26.

8. Jack J. Nelson, Stuart B. Palonsky, and Mary Rose McCarthy, *Critical Issues in Education: Dialogues and Dialectics* (Boston: McGraw-Hill, 2004), 235.

9. William Hayes, *Are We Still a Nation at Risk Two Decades Later?* (Lanham, Md.: Scarecrow Education, 2004), viii.

10. U.S. Department of Education, The National Commission on Excellence in Education, "Introduction," *A Nation at Risk: The Imperative for Educational Reform* (Washington, D.C., April 1983), 6.

11. U.S. Department of Education, "Introduction," *A Nation at Risk*, 2.

12. Diane Ravitch, *Left Back: A Century of Battles over School Reform* (New York: Touchstone, 2000), 411–12.

13. Myra Pollack Sadker and David Miller Sadker, *Teachers, Schools, and Society* (Boston: McGraw-Hill, 2003), 149.

14. Margaret A. Jorgensen and Jenny Hoffmann, *History of the No Child Left Behind Act of 2001* (San Antonio, Tex.: Harcourt Assessment, 2003), www.harcourtassessment.com.

15. Jorgensen and Hoffmann, *History of the No Child Left Behind Act.*

16. Patrick J. McGuinn, *No Child Left Behind and the Transformation of Federal Education Policy, 1965–2005* (Lawrence: University Press of Kansas, 2006), 149.

17. Andrew Rudalevige, "The Politics of No Child Left Behind," *Education Next* 3, no. 4 (2003): www.hoover.org/publications/ednext/3346601.html.

18. David Schuman, *American Schools, American Teachers* (Boston: Pearson, 2004), 244.

19. David Schuman, *American Schools, American Teachers*, 244.

20. L. Dean Webb, *The History of American Education* (Upper Saddle River, N.J.: Pearson, 2006), 360.

21. Ken Goodman et al., eds., *Saving Our Schools* (Berkeley, Calif.: RDR Books, 2004), 3.

22. Deborah Meier et al., *Many Children Left Behind* (Boston: Beacon Press, 2004), 79–80.

❷

THE LAW

It is extremely difficult to summarize the hundreds of pages of legal language contained in the No Child Left Behind law. The task becomes even more daunting when one also attempts to discuss the extensive regulations developed by the Department of Education to implement the legislation. Even a brief review of the ten titles that make up the law would tend to be confusing and perhaps less than helpful as each title contains a number of separate initiatives. As a result, this chapter attempts to simplify the legislation by merely summarizing the significant aspects of the law.

Perhaps the best place to begin is to consider the primary goals of No Child Left Behind. In a speech in 2002, President Bush stated that the purpose of the law is to ensure that "every child in every school must be performing at grade level in the basic subjects that are the key to all learning, reading and math."[1] In the same speech, he argues that "it's an exciting time for American education; it really is. We're facing challenges, but we have the blueprint for success. The No Child Left Behind Act starts the way for a better tomorrow."[2] President Bush's first secretary of education, Rod Paige, claimed that the focus of the law "is to see every child in America—regardless of ethnicity, income, or background—achieve high standards."[3]

Scott Franklin Abernathy, in his excellent book *No Child Left Behind and the Public Schools*, sees the law as changing the objective of what the federal role should be in the field of education. The federal government is no longer seeking to help only children with special needs, such as special education students or children from poor families. Instead it is attempting to ensure that all children have an equally good education. More than that, it is saying that all children will achieve high educational outcomes as measured by mandated tests.[4] In fact, the law states that by the 2013–2014 school year, all children in the United States must reach "world class standards."[5]

Although there are some who do not believe that it is the responsibility of the federal government to improve schools, it is unlikely that anyone would quarrel with the objectives of the law. On the other hand, many would agree with the sentiment expressed in the book *NCLB Meets School Realities*, which suggests that "the devil is in the details." It is certainly true that "the law includes a very complex structure of changes in educational policy and a number of features that turned out to be deeply controversial."[6] Before examining the many concerns and criticisms that have emerged, beginning almost immediately after its passage, it is important that we consider the most significant initiative contained in the law.

Prior to the passage of No Child Left Behind, all of the states had federally approved state curriculum standards (what children must know and be able to do) in the areas of language arts, mathematics, and science. The new law mandated that by the 2005–2006 school year, schools were to administer federally approved tests in language arts and math in grades three through eight. Requiring a test at each of these grade levels went beyond what most states had been doing. Science tests were mandated at the elementary, middle school or junior high, and high school level by the 2006–2007 school year.[7]

To ensure that the test results would give a complete picture of how various children were doing in a school district, the test scores must be reported in eight different subgroups. The first five are ethnic groups. The categories are white, black, Hispanic, American Indian, and Asian or Pacific Islanders. In addition, there is separate reporting for students eligible for free or reduced-price lunches, those with limited English proficiency, and those qualifying for special education services.[8]

The results of all of the tests, including the scores of each subgroup, must then be made known to the public. While all of the states had already developed testing programs that required public accountability, No Child Left Behind went far beyond what was already occurring. The law placed great significance on what it called the "proficiency level" on the state tests.[9] To measure whether or not a school was meeting an appropriate proficiency level, the legislation introduced the yardstick known as "adequate yearly progress." Sanctions are placed on schools that fail to reach the appropriate adequate yearly progress milestones. When a school fails to make adequate yearly progress, the consequences become increasingly more serious each consecutive year.

A school must reach its assigned goal in each of the student categories listed above or be considered to not have met the adequate yearly progress requirement. A second consecutive year of failure in any group causes the school to be publicly labeled "in need of improvement." If one of its schools has received this designation, a district is mandated to develop a "professional improvement plan." It is also required that at least 10 percent of federal money going to such schools must be used for professional development and any plans created must be based on "scientifically validated educational research." Parents with children in schools that are labeled "in need of improvement" are notified of the failure and allowed to transfer their child to a successful school within the district.

A third consecutive year of failing to achieve adequate yearly progress results in the continuation of the conditions imposed the previous year, along with the mandate that the district provide supplementary educational services to the students in the failing categories.[10] These supplementary tutoring services are chosen by the parent and can include programs offered by the local public-school district, as well as alternatives such as those offered by private companies and even "faith-based" groups.[11]

After the fourth consecutive year in which a school fails to meet its adequate yearly progress goal, NCLB requires that the district take serious "corrective action." The alternatives may include "replacing staff, overhauling the curriculum, reducing management authority at the local level, hiring outside experts, or lengthening the school day and/or year." If these measures do not remedy the problem, after the fifth year, a plan for restructuring the school must be submitted to the federal government. This plan must either reconstitute the school as a charter school, replace all or most school personnel, allow the school to be run by a private management firm, or have the state intervene to take appropriate measures. After a sixth consecutive year of failure to meet adequate yearly progress goals, the restructuring plan is carried out.[12]

At each of these stages, the public in the school district is made aware of the sanctions placed on the school. This accountability is meant to force school officials to take seriously the need to meet the educational needs of all children. Both teachers and school administrators cannot help but be aware that the results of the mandated tests could greatly affect them professionally and might even cause them to lose their jobs. Supporters of this system argue that since the 1965 passage of the Elementary Secondary Education Act, billions of dollars have been spent that have not brought about higher test scores, especially for nonwhite poor children, and so a dramatic change in the law was necessary.

As additional motivation for public schools to do better, No Child Left Behind sets aside money to establish charter schools to compete with the traditional schools within a district. These schools are given freedom from many state regulations and are allowed more flexibility in meeting the educational objectives established by the law. For example, charter schools might not have to hire all state-certified teachers. They have additional flexibility in the area of curriculum, the length of the school year or school day, and, in most states, do not have to deal with the teacher unions in their district. The whole thrust of the charter movement is to release these schools from bureaucratic restrictions and allow them the freedom to experiment. While most of the more than 3,600 charter schools are located in large suburban or urban districts, the total number continues to increase each year.

Although charter schools might have flexibility in who they hire as teachers and administrators, traditional public schools are given less freedom in selecting their professional personnel. No Child Left Behind requires that schools have only "highly qualified teachers." The original legislation required that this provision be met by the 2005–2006 school year. In most states, "highly qualified" has meant that the teachers should be "fully licensed or certified by the state" in which they teach. Elementary teachers in all states are required to have earned a bachelor's degree along with passing a rigorous test that covers all areas of the curriculum. Instructors at the middle school and high school level need to pass a "rigorous test in the subject areas they are teaching."[13] Because many districts have been unable to meet these qualifications, the federal Education Department has extended the deadline several times. In doing so, the department has required the states to develop a plan for how they will meet the requirement to have only fully certified teachers in their traditional public schools.

There are a number of other important aspects of the law, which are listed in the executive summary published by the Department of Education. These include the following:

More flexibility for states and local educational agencies in the use of federal education dollars: The law gives states and school districts "unprecedented flexibility in the use of federal education funds in exchange for strong accountability for results."

A stronger emphasis on reading, especially with the youngest children: A new Reading First grant program is included in the legislation. School districts that are successful in gaining one of these grants can use the money to assist children in kindergarten through third grade who are at risk of reading failure. The grants also provide professional development opportunities in the field of reading instruction for teachers of kindergarten through third grade.

New Improving Teacher Quality State Grants: These grants focus on providing assistance to schools in utilizing "scientifically based research to prepare, train, and recruit high-quality teachers."

Assistance for states and local districts in providing safe, drug-free schools: "States must allow students who attend a persistently dangerous school or who are victims of violent crime at school to transfer to a safe school."[14]

In addition, an initiative titled Reading First provided money to states and districts to establish "scientific, research-based" reading programs for children in kindergarten through third grade. The law allowed flexibility to districts to "transfer up to 50 percent of the money from several major Elementary Secondary Education Act programs." There was also the possibility that up to 150 districts could gain an agreement with the federal Department of Education to consolidate all of their Elementary Secondary Education Act programs, excluding Title I. The purpose of these provisions was to give states and local districts additional flexibility in spending their federal funds.[15]

For most of the Democrats who voted for the law, the single most important aspect of the legislation was the dramatic increase of funding that was included in the initial passage. In the 2002 federal budget there was an increase of 18 percent from the prior year in Title I grants and a 17 percent overall increase in aid to elementary and secondary education. Problems occurred, however, when in subsequent years the president's proposed budget sought much smaller increases. For example, in 2004, even though Congress increased appropriations beyond what was requested by the president, the overall increase for education was only 5.1 percent. Had the president's proposed 2004 budget been adopted, it would have decreased appropriations for elementary and secondary education by 2.6 percent.[16]

As the cost of the war in Iraq continued to increase, domestic programs such as federal aid to education did not receive what supporters believed was necessary. As we shall see, this funding issue has been a significant problem, which has been raised by critics of the law. This is especially true because meeting the mandates of No Child Left Behind has proven to be quite costly to both state governments and local school districts. Because of the cost, as well as other additional burdens imposed by the law, there has been a negative response from many quarters. While some states and local districts might consider ignoring No Child Left Behind, they are well aware that such a decision would lead to a loss of federal aid. It is the money in large part that has caused schools and states to move forward in attempting to meet the requirements of No Child Left Behind. In the next chapter, we will consider the events that have affected the law during the past five years.

NOTES

1. Mary E. Williams, ed., *Education: Opposing Viewpoints* (Detroit: Thomson Gale, 2005), 156.

2. Williams, *Education: Opposing Viewpoints*, 161.

3. Margaret A. Jorgensen and Jenny Hoffmann, *History of the No Child Left Behind Act of 2001* (San Antonio, Tex.: Harcourt Assessment, 2003), www.harcourtassessment.com.

4. Scott Franklin Abernathy, *No Child Left Behind and the Public Schools* (Ann Arbor: University of Michigan Press, 2007), 2–3.

5. Ken Goodman et al., eds., *Saving Our Schools* (Berkeley, Calif.: RDR Books, 2004), 12.

6. Gail Sunderman, James S. Kim, and Gary Orfield, *NCLB Meets School Realities* (Thousand Oaks, Calif.: Sage Publications, 2005), xxvi.

7. Patrick J. McGuinn, *No Child Left Behind and the Transformation of Federal Education Policy, 1965–2005* (Lawrence: University Press of Kansas, 2006), 180.

8. Abernathy, *No Child Left Behind and the Public Schools*, 5.

9. Sunderman, Kim, and Orfield, *NCLB Meets School Realities*, xxix.

10. Abernathy, *No Child Left Behind and the Public Schools*, 8.

11. Sunderman, Kim, and Orfield, *NCLB Meets School Realities*, 59.

12. Abernathy, *No Child Left Behind and the Public Schools*, 8.

13. James A. Johnson et al., *Foundations of American Education* (Boston: Pearson, 2005), 157.

14. U.S. Department of Education, "Executive Summary of the No Child Left Behind Act of 2001," www.ed.gov/nclb/overview/intro/execsumm.html (accessed 9 July 2004).

15. McGuinn, *No Child Left Behind and the Transformation of Federal Education Policy*, 80–81.

16. Sunderman, Kim, and Orfield, *NCLB Meets School Realities*, 10.

❸

THE FIRST FIVE YEARS

Despite the bipartisan support for No Child Left Behind, it has been the source of significant controversy during its early years. Even before the law was signed by the president, an editorial in the *Wall Street Journal* expressed disappointment with the compromises that had been necessary to secure its passage. The editors wrote in the December 19, 2001, issue that "politically, however, the bill looks like a compromise in which the GOP traded more money—an $8 billion increase in spending—in return for a signing ceremony that will give it higher approval ratings on education. That's nice for Republicans, but it doesn't mean much for kids."[1]

For the official signing ceremony in January 2002, President Bush arranged a ten-hour trip that saw him traveling to three different states. Along with the president were four of the congressional leaders who helped bring about the final passage of the bill. Among them were Republican Congressman John A. Boehner and Democratic Senator Edward Kennedy. An examination of some of the newspaper accounts of these signing ceremonies finds that the reporters tended to emphasize the personalities involved and the political implications rather than the specifics of the law. For example, the *New York Times* story, which was headlined *Focusing on the Home Front, Bush Signs Education*

Bill, highlighted the signing at Boston Latin, the nation's oldest public school. The article noted that "Mr. Bush and Mr. Kennedy, scions of the nation's two most famous and opposing political families with much to gain from each other, took time in each of their speeches . . . for extravagant compliments."[2]

It is important to remember that the No Child Left Behind law was agreed upon just a few months after the 9/11 attacks. For a short period, the president and Congress were working together both in the area of foreign policy and domestic legislation. It is also true that politicians, including the president, were already thinking about the politics of the 2002 congressional elections. Later on the day of the signing, at Hamilton High School in Hamilton, Ohio, the president attempted to combine the national concern about the war on terror and our education problems when he said, "We're going to win the war overseas and we need to win the war against literacy [*sic*] here at home as well."[3] The *Houston Chronicle* highlighted in its story the president's comment that "we've spent billions of dollars with lousy results. . . . Now it's time to spend billions of dollars and get good results."[4]

After the president signed the law, there was still much to do. Even though the bill contained over 1,200 pages, there was still the need for the Education Department to draw up the administrative guidelines necessary to implement the law. The evening following the signing ceremony, Rod Paige, the former superintendent of schools in Houston, who had been appointed by the president as secretary of education, gathered together thirty state chief education officers and made clear to them what was to be his department's policy concerning the enforcement of No Child Left Behind. States were going to be expected to meet all of the conditions of the law as well as the regulations developed by the department. He warned that there were not going to be waivers and that noncompliance would result in the imposition of the appropriate penalties.[5]

For the most part, Secretary Paige indeed took a hard line in enforcing the law. The regulations prepared by the Department of Education to enforce the law had a different emphasis from the previous rules. Schools were to be held accountable for all children and failure would bring significant consequences to those school districts which failed to meet the guideline known as "adequate yearly progress." This requirement, along with many additional mandates, caused state education officials and school administrators to become overwhelmed in their efforts to understand all that was involved in attempting to meet the requirements of No Child Left Behind.

Consultants emerged who were hired to help explain the law. Some larger districts created new administrative positions and gave to these individuals the job of introducing and enforcing the law within their school systems. At the state level, groups were formed to develop new tests. Although every state had already developed examinations for certain grades in language arts and math, it was necessary now to have tests for students in grades three through eight. In addition, every state and school district had to evaluate its reading programs to determine if they were based on scientifically based research. All of these tasks cost additional money, and very quickly it was being suggested that Washington was not providing adequate financing to pay for the total cost of compliance.

By spring 2003, additional controversy emerged when Secretary Paige warned the states that they should not lower the educational standards of their tests to ensure that they were meeting the adequate yearly progress guidelines.[7] As the most vocal defender of the law, Secretary Paige was also responsible for becoming involved in a highly publicized quarrel with the nation's largest teacher organization, the National Education Association. Although he would later apologize for the remark, the secretary found himself quoted in the *New York Times* calling the group a "terrorist organization."[8]

He was not alone in reacting strongly to the initial attempts to change the regulations. Republican Congressman John A. Boehner, one of the major architects of the final version of the law, charged that the critics would "gut" the law and "make it easier for states to go back to hiding the fact that some children are being denied a quality education, even as those states accept billions in increased federal education funds."[9]

By 2003, there were numerous groups and individuals who were keeping the Bush administration on the defensive as the Department of Education attempted to enforce the law. Perhaps the single biggest problem was funding. While in the first year there was a dramatic increase in aid to education, in every year since then there has been strong criticism to what many considered inadequate funding for carrying out the many mandates required. Democrats were very vocal in faulting the administration for turning away from what they believed had been a firm commitment for significant amounts of new money for the schools. The issue was brought to the public's attention in the 2004 presidential election. Senator Kennedy, whose support had made the passage of No Child Left Behind possible, charged during the campaign that "President Bush thinks he is providing enough for schools. Parents, teachers, and I don't."[10]

John Kerry, Kennedy's fellow senator from Massachusetts and the Democratic candidate for president, echoed his friend's sentiments when he charged that schoolchildren were being neglected in order to fund the president's tax cuts for the rich. The funding issue came to the forefront again in 2006, when President Bush requested only $13.3 billion of the $22.75 billion that was authorized under the law.[11]

The lack of money to finance No Child Left Behind was only one of a number of problems that have emerged. One month after the 2004 presidential election, "a coalition of 30 national organizations called on Congress to make major changes in the law, including how academic progress is measured, substitution of sanctions that do not have a consistent record of success, and a funding increase."[12] Until the resignation of Secretary Paige, the Department of Education appeared to be less than open to suggestions for changing the regulations. Initially, his replacement, Margaret Spellings, appeared more willing to consider modifications. For example, the provision that established a deadline for all schools to have "highly qualified" teachers by the 2005–2006 school year has been extended each year. While this has occurred, the department has required that the extensions were "contingent on evidence that a state had been reordering its priorities and building the systems needed to take responsibility for the quality of its teaching force." In addition, the states were mandated to provide an approved plan for meeting the requirement.[13]

Although Secretary Spellings appeared to be more open than her predecessor, the law itself was still being challenged by state legislatures, national teacher unions, and individual school districts. When school opened in 2005, forty-seven states were in some "stage of rebellion" against specific portions of the law. At the same point in time, in twenty states there had been at least some discussion of opting out of some or all of the mandates. This was being considered even though the states would lose considerable funding. The state of Connecticut had filed a major lawsuit charging that the federal government was providing insufficient funding to meet the new mandates.[14]

Like Secretary Paige, Margaret Spellings has also created controversy. An example would be an editorial in the *Seattle Times* titled "Spellings' Errors." The author suggested that the education secretary deserved "to be read the riot act when she appears this week before a congressional committee probing allegations of mismanagement and cronyism in the Reading First program." The editorial goes on to charge that six billion dollars allotted to improve reading scores in disadvantaged schools "appears to have served as a profit center for textbook authors and education consultants with ties to the Bush administration." Both Congress and the Department of Education's inspector general are investigating some of the transactions for possible criminal review.[15] In a first-page article in *Education Week*, the chairman of the House Education and Labor Committee, Representative George Miller, is quoted as saying, "it is clear that—at a minimum—the Education Department's oversight failures have been monumental."[16] Along with some very bad press, there has been less than enthusiastic support given to the law by important segments of the educational community.

Despite their lack of enthusiasm for the law, there has been a growing recognition by many organizations that No Child Left Behind is likely to be reauthorized. Even after being critical during the first five years of No Child Left Behind, the National Education Association, by 2007, was not suggesting that the law be scrapped. Instead, it appeared to be the group's position that the goals of the law were indeed "laudable" but that it must be "fundamentally improved" and that "federal lawmakers need to provide adequate funding."[17]

The American Federation of Teachers, a smaller but still very powerful union of teachers, has addressed the law in this way:

> Flaws in the law are undercutting its original promise. Guidance for states has been unclear, untimely and unhelpful, and the U.S. Department of Education's attempts to make the law more flexible have

brought about only minimal improvements without addressing NCLB's larger flaws. Underlying all these issues is the pervasive problem of funding, which is far less than what was promised and far less than what is needed.[18]

Despite its reservations, this group, too, has not officially called for scrapping the law in seeking changes in the law during the reauthorization process.

The National School Boards Association, which was vocal in its criticism of No Child Left Behind, has also joined in the effort to affect the reauthorization process. After its national convention in July 2007, the group submitted to members of the House Education and Labor Committee 400 resolutions written by school boards across the country. Each of these resolutions represented a proposal to alter the legislation. At the same time, the national organization had developed its official position on the law, which calls for forty changes.[19]

The National Middle School Association, after agreeing with the basic goal of the No Child Left Behind Act, has stated that "we do not believe the legislation fully addresses the needs of students in grades five through eight." This organization seems to accept the fact that the law will continue, and it has also submitted recommendations for change.[20]

Perhaps the single best indication of the position of a variety of groups can be found in the "Joint Organizational Statement on No Child Left Behind (NCLB) Act." By July 2007, 138 interested organizations had signed a document stating that:

> The undersigned education, civil rights, religious, children's disability, civic and labor organizations are committed to the No Child Left Behind Act's objectives of strong academic achievement for all children and closing the achievement gap. We believe that the federal government has a critical role to play in attaining these goals. We endorse the use of an accountability system that helps ensure all children, including children of color, from low-income families, with disabilities, and of limited English proficiency, are prepared to be successful, participating members of our democracy.
>
> While we all have different positions on various aspects of the law, based on concerns raised during the implementation of NCLB, we believe the following significant, constructive corrections are among

those necessary to make the Act fair and effective. Among these concerns are: over-emphasizing standardized testing; narrowing curriculum and instruction to focus on test preparation rather than richer academic learning; over-identifying schools in need of improvement; using sanctions that do not improve schools; inappropriately excluding low-scoring children in order to boost test results; and inadequate funding. Overall, the law's emphasis needs to shift from applying sanctions for failing to raise test scores to holding states and localities accountable for making the systematic changes that improve student achievement.[21]

The groups signing this statement included such powerful and diverse organizations as the American Civil Liberties Union, American Federation of Labor-Congress of Industrial Organizations, Association for Supervision and Curriculum Development, Association of Teacher Educators, National Association for the Advancement of Colored People, National Association of Secondary School Principals, and the National Rural Education Association.[22]

While it would seem that there is significant national support for reauthorizing No Child Left Behind with changes, there are those who question whether or not the law can be made acceptable. A leading voice for conservatives, *Human Events.com*, quoted a Congressman, James DeMint, who voted against the law, claiming that "No Child Left Behind started with some good ideas, but what Congress didn't mess up, the bureaucracy has messed up—There is so much absurdity now within No Child Left Behind that it's going to be difficult to tweak it and fix it. We need to look at a way to allow states to get out of it in a way that would let them do it responsibly."[23] If states were allowed to ignore the law, it is very possible that some would choose to do so. It is even more likely that they would consider the option if they could do so and still receive federal aid.

Others, including Democratic presidential candidate Bill Richardson, have gone further by stating that the law should be "scrapped."[24] Of more concern to the supporters of the law than the position of a single presidential candidate was a public opinion survey concerning the future of No Child Left Behind. The study found that among parents of children in kindergarten through grade twelve, 36 percent believed that there was a need for "major changes" in the law and 13 percent believed that it should not be reauthorized. Among public school teachers, 58 percent favored major changes, while an alarming 25 percent believed that it should not be reauthorized. The response of public school administrators was only slightly more supportive of the legislation.[25]

As Congress began to debate the future of the law, it appeared that although there was considerable controversy and significant opposition to its reauthorization, the predominant sentiment seemed to be that with major changes, No Child Left Behind should be renewed. It also was true that Lynn Olson, writing in *Education Week*, was correct when she stated that "despite ongoing complaints, the federal No Child Left Behind Act has become implanted in the culture of America's public school system."[26] With this reality in mind, and before considering the data available concerning the successes and failures of the law to date, it would seem helpful to summarize the concerns that have arisen during the last five years. This will be the topic of chapter 4.

NOTES

1. "Education Hoopla," *Wall Street Journal*, 19 December 2001.

2. Elisabeth Bumiller, "Focusing on Home Front, Bush Signs Education Bill," *New York Times*, 9 January 2002.

3. Bumiller, "Focusing on Home Front."

4. "Pledging to Beat Illiteracy, Bush Signs $26 Billion Legislation," *Houston Chronicle*, 9 Jan, 2002, 3 star edition.

5. Patrick J. McGuinn, *No Child Left Behind and the Transformation of Federal Education Policy, 1965–2005* (Lawrence: University Press of Kansas, 2006), 183.

6. U.S. Department of Education, "Executive Summary of the No Child Left Behind Act of 2001," www.ed.gov/nclb/overview/intro/execsumm.html (accessed 27 July 2007).

7. Andrew Rudalevige, "The Politics of No Child Left Behind," *Education Next* 3, no. 4 (2003): www.hoover.org/publications/ednext/3346601.html.

8. Sam Dillon, "Education Chief Again Apologizes for 'Terrorist Remark,'" *New York Times*, 2 March 2004, www.nytimes.com/2004/03/02/politics/02PAIG .html.

9. Diana Jean Schemo, "14 States Ask U.S. to Revise Some Education Law Rules," *The New York Times*, 25 March 2004, www.nytimes.com/2004/03/25/education/25CHIL.html.

10. CNN.com, "Bush Makes Money, Touts Education," *Inside Politics*, 6 January 2004, www.cnn.com/2004/AllPolitics/01/06/elec04.prez.bush.fundraising.ap/index.html.

11. "No Child Left Behind Act," *Wikipedia*, en.wikipedia.org/wiki/No_Child_Left_Behind_Act (accessed 25 June 2007).

12. Lynn Olson, "Taking Root," *Education Week*, 8 December 2004, www.edweek.org/ew/articles/2004/12/08/15nclb/1.h24.html.

13. Bess Keller, "States Given Extra Year on Teachers," *Education Week*, 2 November 2005, www.edweek.org/ew/articles/2005/11/02/10reprieve.h25.html.

14. Jason Szep, "Bush Faces Growing Revolt over Education Policy," Reuters, 2 September 2005, www.signonsandiego.com/news/education/20050902-0805-education-reform.html.

15. "Spellings' Errors," *Seattle Times*, 7 May 2007, seattletimes.nwsource.com/html/editorialsopinion/2003693989_readed07.html.

16. Kathleen Kennedy Manzo, "Senate Report Cites 'Reading First' Conflicts," *Education Week*, 16 May 2007, 24.

17. National Education Association, "No Child Left Behind Act/ESEA," www.nea.org/esea/policy.html (accessed 27 July 2007).

18. American Federation of Teachers, "NCLB—Let's Get It Right," www.aft.org/topics/nclb/index.htm (accessed 27 July 2007).

19. National School Boards Association, "Nearly 400 Local School Board Resolutions Delivered to Capitol Hill Urging Congress to Reauthorize the No Child Left Behind Act," 18 July 2007, www.susanohania.org/show_nclb_outrages.html?id=3000 (accessed 16 April 2008).

20. National Middle School Association, "NCLB Recommendations," www.nmsa.org/portals/0/pdf/advocacy/messages/NMSA_NCLB_Recommendations.pdf.

21. FairTest, "Joint Organizational Statement on No Child Left Behind (NCLB) Act," 21 October 2004 (list of 138 signers updated 18 July 2007), www.fairtest.org/joint-organizational-statement-no-child-left-behind (accessed 27 July 2007).

22. FairTest, "Joint Organizational Statement."

23. Robert B. Bluey, "A Conservative Alternative to No Child Left Behind," *Human Events.com*, 13 March 2007, www.humanevents.com/article.php?id=19777.

24. Bill Richardson, "A Champion for Quality Education," www.richardson forpresident.com/issues/page?id=0003 (accessed 14 August 2007).

25. Howard Blume, "Parents, Educators Split on What to Do with No Child Left Behind," *Los Angeles Times*, 20 June 2007, California metro section.

26. Lynn Olson, "Taking Root.

4

THE CRITICS

The reasons for criticizing No Child Left Behind range from significant philosophical differences to concerns about specific technical aspects of the legislation.

There are those who feel that the law is taking our schools in the wrong direction. For over 100 years, there has been a major conflict between those educators who favor a traditional approach to teaching and learning and another group who are in favor of what has been labeled "progressive education." The most prominent early progressive was John Dewey, who rebelled against the traditional methods used in schools. He opposed a centrally developed curriculum and wished to create classrooms where students and teachers had significant flexibility.

For progressives, children learn best by being actively engaged in the process. For them, instead of merely passing on information, an instructor should be a facilitator who provides students with practical learning experiences. Such approaches as individual and group projects as well as field trips are essential in a progressive classroom.

For those who are philosophically supportive of progressive education, No Child Left Behind, with its emphasis on state-mandated learning standards and high-stakes testing, has greatly curtailed the ability of individual teachers to provide meaningful educational experiences. Many teachers are having difficulty dealing with the pressure to prepare children for the tests. Two typical examples are the following e-mails that I received from former students who have been teaching for several years. When asked about the effect of the law on their teaching they wrote the following:

> NCLB has a great impact on me and my fellow teachers. It has really zapped the creativity out of our classrooms. We no longer have the time to do all the hands-on activities that we used to, but now have had to dedicate all our time to test prep in an endeavor to try to get scores up. It has been a nightmare this year, honestly. We are all so glad to have the ELA and Math tests over. NCLB is certainly leaving kids behind. . . . I can't tell you how many kids just can't do those tests. They have made tremendous gains this year, but still can't pass the tests.[1]

> As for No Child Left Behind . . . I'd be lying if I said that I didn't hate the tests. Not a day goes by where I don't hear a colleague mention about having to cover something in time for "the test." There's hardly any time for fun. We even work through our snack time . . . and we don't have recess. No one told us that we can't go outside . . . we just don't have time to go. It's sad.[2]

The concerns of these young teachers are shared by many educators. A prominent progressive, Deborah Meier, believes that schools should be smaller and self-governing. Rather than a mandated state curriculum and tests, she believes "that every school must have the power and the responsibility to select and design its own particulars." Meier contends that the "top down" reforms called for in the No Child Left Behind legislation are doomed to failure.[3]

A more radical view of what traditional education and federal mandates are doing can be found in the writings of John Holt. For him, most schools have got it all wrong.

> Behind much of what we do in school lie some ideas that could be expressed roughly as follows: (1) Of the vast body of human knowledge, there are certain bits and pieces that can be called essential. . . . (2) the extent to which a person can be considered educated . . . depends on the amount of this essential knowledge that he carries about with him; (3) it is

the duty of schools, therefore, to get as much of this essential knowledge as possible into the minds of children. . . . These ideas are absurd and harmful nonsense. . . . Children quickly forget all but a small part of what they learn in school. It is of no use or interest to them; they do not want, or expect, or even intend to remember it. The only difference between bad and good students in this respect is that bad students forget right away while the good students are careful to wait until after the exam.[4]

More recently, a number of authors have written books that describe the negative impact of the law on what is occurring in our schools. Interested readers could find in their bookstores titles such as *Many Children Left Behind: How the No Child Left Behind Act Is Damaging Our Children and Our Schools*, and *Saving Our Schools: The Case for Public Education Saying No to "No Child Left Behind."* The thrust of the progressive argument, perhaps, can be best understood by considering the words of Alfie Kohn, who wrote in an article published in the *Washington Post* that:

> The best kind of teaching takes its cue from the understanding that people are active learners. In such a classroom, students are constantly making decisions, becoming participants in their own education. Each is part of a community of learners, coming to understand ideas from the inside out with one another's help. They still acquire facts and skills, but in a context, and for a purpose. Their questions drive the curriculum. Learning to think like scientists and historians matters more than memorizing lists of definitions and dates.[5]

While progressive educators have been outspoken in their opposition to the law and will most likely oppose its reauthorization, their influence outside of the educational community is limited.

Another group of opponents are in a much better position to affect the reauthorization process. At the time of the original passage in 2002, there were many conservatives in Congress, state government, and on local boards of education who were strongly opposed to additional involvement by the federal government in the field of education. Mostly Republicans, they pointed to the fact that the Constitution seems to reserve the field of education for the states and local government. They also noted that until the middle of the twentieth century, this was the reality in our country. These individuals believe that the federal government has merely created a wasteful bureaucracy in the field of education and they will continue to oppose the whole idea of No Child Left Behind.

While there are those who strongly oppose the federal government's increasing role in public schools, there are also important national leaders who believe that Washington needs to be even more involved. When No Child Left Behind was passed, conservatives insisted that the curriculum and the tests be developed at the state level. As we shall see, this decision has created fifty different sets of curriculum standards and examinations. Because of this, it is extremely difficult, if not impossible, to compare educational progress among the states. State examinations vary in difficulty from one state to another. During the original debates about the law, many Democrats supported the idea of national standards and tests. This will undoubtedly be part of the discussions concerning reauthorization.

The impetus for creating national standards was dramatically demonstrated when two former Republican secretaries of education, William J. Bennett and Rod Paige, wrote in the *Washington Post* an op-ed titled "Why We Need a National School Test." They charged that allowing states to create their own standards and tests was "working badly." In support of the need for change, they referred to a Fordham Foundation report that demonstrates "that most states have deployed mediocre standards, and there's increasing evidence that some are playing games with their tests and accountability systems." After giving examples of what is happening at the state level, the authors concluded that, "Washington should set sound national academic standards and administer a high-quality national test."[6] Any discussion of national standards and tests will be extremely controversial and would face opposition from many fronts. The chance that the idea will be included as part of this reauthorization seems remote.

The criticisms of state manipulation of tests have been frequent during the past several years. One way to evaluate how states are meeting the requirements of the law is to compare the scores of students in the federally funded National Assessment of Educational Progress test with what the states have submitted concerning their own examinations. There are states that have claimed that 80–90 percent of their students are proficient in reading and math, while the na tional tests set the proficiency figure at 30 percent.[7] Bennett and Paige, in their op-ed, cite the example of Tennessee, which reported that based on its state tests, "87 percent of its fourth-graders are 'proficient' in reading." The results for students in Tennessee on the National Assessment of Educational Progress test set the number at 27 percent. In Oklahoma, the state's list of schools that need improvement "dropped by 85 percent—not because they improved or their students learned more, but because a bureaucrat in the state's education department changed the way Oklahoma calculates 'adequate yearly progress' under the federal law."[8]

While some states are working to ensure that the vast majority of their schools are not penalized under the law, there is still the fear in many districts that their schools will face dire consequences for failing to meet the adequate yearly progress standards. CNN broadcast a story in June 2007 titled "Thousands of Failing Schools Face Major Overhaul." It reported that approximately "2,300 individual schools are either in restructuring or a year away from planning such drastic action." Under the law, this could include firing the principal and making significant changes in the faculty and curriculum. For superintendent of schools John Deasy in Prince Edward, Maryland, "this is life and death." Many of the schools being identified are in poor urban areas, and in these districts raising test scores is a difficult educational challenge.[9]

Urban administrators are not the only ones critical of the high-stakes testing mandates of No Child Left Behind. W. James Popham, a leading authority on student assessment, has written extensively about the weaknesses in testing procedures in the United States. In his book *America's "Failing" Schools*, he lists the "harmful consequences of educational mismeasurement." This discussion begins with a description of a trend he calls "curricular reductionism." Here the concern is that any subject that is not tested under the law will receive less attention than language arts, math, and science.[10] In one poll, 44 percent of the schools surveyed admitted that they were reducing the time being used for teaching subjects other than language arts and math. The poll found that 36 percent of districts reduced the time spent on social studies and 16 percent reduced time devoted to art and music.[11]

Popham writes that the second consequence of the testing program is "excessive test preparation." In some classrooms, large blocks of time are used to drill students on possible test questions and also on teaching effective test-taking techniques. He also suggests that some teachers engage in "unethical test preparation practices." Specifically, he charges that children are being drilled on "practice exercises consisting of items very similar to a test's actual items or, in some instances, the actual items themselves. Along with those practice items, teachers typically supply students with their very own correct answer keys."[12] There have been a number of stories that have also implicated school administrators in schemes for improving the test results reported to Washington.

Popham's final criticism is the contention that many states are using "unsuitable tests for evaluating schools." He is especially critical of those who use "nationally standardized, off-the-shelf achievement tests." While admitting that it is possible to develop "appropriate standardized achievement tests" that can provide "accountability evidence," Popham concludes that the "standards-based assessment" approach that is inherent in the No Child Left Behind regulations has "flopped."[13]

An article appearing in *Education Week* in 2007 highlights another possible negative development resulting from No Child Left Behind. The author, Debra Viadero, focuses on a study done by two professors from the University of Chicago. The conclusion in the study is that many schools are concentrating on the middle-level or "bubble kids." These are students who with extra help might reach the necessary proficiency level to help schools reach their adequate yearly progress goals. In concentrating on these children, it would appear that teachers are paying less attention to low achievers, who have little chance of reaching proficiency, as well as gifted students who do not need additional help to pass the tests.[14]

Paying more attention to the middle-level students, in the long run, will not help schools meet the primary objective of the law, which states that by 2014, all students that are tested (which must be at least 95 percent of the students in any school) will reach grade level in reading and math. Many have scoffed at this objective, arguing that it will always be a goal that is impossible to achieve. Robert L. Linn, co-director of the National Center for Research on Evaluation, Standards, and Student Testing at University of California–Los Angeles, has been quoted as saying that "there is zero percent chance that we will ever reach a 100 percent target . . . but because the title of the law is so rhetorically brilliant, politicians are afraid to change this completely unrealistic standard. They don't want to be accused of leaving some children behind."[15]

Fairfax County Superintendent Jack Dale went even further when he stated that it was "'absurd' to expect total proficiency, especially when federal officials require immigrant children who have been in U.S. schools for little more than a year to meet the standard."[16] Along with criticisms of the unrealistic goals and the overemphasis on testing, there are other aspects of the law which have come under fire.

A number of educators engaged in educational research have faulted Congress for paying too little attention to what researchers have found to be true about the best ways to increase student learning. Professor Gary Orfield, of Harvard University, helped to prepare a report after the passage of the law titled *Hard Work for Good Schools: Facts Not Fads*. The report suggests that the authors of No Child Left Behind in Washington failed to adequately consult with the educational research community when they drafted the law and the enforcement regulations. As a result, what was enacted was "mostly the fads." Orfield also faults the legislation for allotting so little money to support educational research.[17]

Others have taken issue with the provision of the law that mandates that all students be taught by a "highly qualified teacher." Such a person must have "a bachelor's degree from a four-year college, a state teacher's license, and demonstrated competency in the subject being taught." Accomplishing this mandate can be especially difficult in small rural schools and in poor urban communities. In a small high school, it might be necessary to have a single teacher assigned to several different science classes. Finding a competent, licensed teacher who can teach physics as well as biology can be extremely challenging. It also has been argued that "without increased funding to improve teacher salaries and working conditions, it is difficult to imagine how nearly two million 'highly qualified' teachers will be drawn to teaching, or even more challenging, stay in teaching."[18] The fact that it has been necessary for the Education Department to extend the deadline for meeting this requirement demonstrates the difficulty involved in this mandate.

There has also been a great deal of debate on the possible negative effect of the law on teachers. PBS brought this issue to the forefront when it highlighted on its nightly news program a three-part series on No Child Left Behind. The third evening of the series focused on a number of teachers, all with excellent professional reputations, who expressed what they felt were significant negative aspects of No Child Left Behind. References were made to teachers who have left the profession as a result of the pressures created by the new mandates. One such teacher, Anthony Cody, spoke with tears in his eyes when he explained why he had left the teaching profession after sixteen years.[19] Such media coverage can only be detrimental as Congress debates the reauthorization of the law.

While the number of individuals leaving teaching because of No Child Left Behind is probably small, the profession already has an alarming drop-out rate. This is especially true for teachers in their first five years in the classroom. Perhaps even more disturbing is the charge that the pressure of the tests is causing more students to drop out of school. Although it is impossible to prove a direct connection between the law and student drop-outs, as a nation, we do have a significant problem with those students failing to complete a high school diploma.

A final complaint about No Child Left Behind is the little-known fact that the law does not cover all schools. Federal financial aid relies on the formula contained in Title I of the Elementary Secondary Education Act, and "10 percent of the school districts in the country did not apply for Title I funds under NCLB. Thus a large number of school districts do not face federal penalties if they do not have highly-qualified teachers in the classroom, or do not meet the quality standards of NCLB."[20] These schools, which are located primarily in wealthy districts, cannot be forced to comply with the law. Title IX of No Child Left Behind also frees all private and home schools from the provisions of the law.[21] Some critics argue that these exemptions are unwise and unfair.

Along with the persistent demands for additional federal funding, all of the criticisms mentioned in this chapter are part of the debate over reauthorizing No Child Left Behind. These and other concerns of educators, parents, and interested citizens will likely lead to some major changes in the law. Before focusing on the discussions in Congress, it would now seem appropriate to look at the results of No Child Left Behind to date. For many reasons, it is difficult to find definitive data that will answer the most fundamental questions regarding the successes and failures of the legislation. Even with these limitations, it is important to attempt to make a fair assessment of what has occurred during the past five years. Since it is a chief objective of No Child Left Behind to improve the reading level of American students, we will begin by considering this essential academic skill.

NOTES

1. Dawn Zegers, e-mail to William Hayes, 19 March 2007.
2. Chelsea Durham, e-mail to William Hayes, 15 October 2007.
3. James W. M. Noll, ed., *Taking Sides* (Guilford, Conn.: McGraw-Hill/Dushkin, 2004), 327.
4. Jack J. Nelson, Stuart B. Palonsky, and Mary Rose McCarthy, *Critical Issues in Education: Dialogues and Dialectics* (Boston: McGraw-Hill, 2004), 235.
5. Alfie Kohn, "A Look at . . . Getting Back to Basics: First Lesson: Unlearn How We Learned," *Washington Post*, 10 October 1999, www.alfiekohn.org/teaching/alagbtb.htm.
6. William J. Bennett and Rod Paige, "Why We Need a National School Test," *Washington Post*, 21 September 2006.
7. Kevin Carey, "Hot Air: How States Inflate Their Educational Progress under NCLB," *Education Sector*, 16 May 2006, www.educationsector.org/analysis/analysis_show.htm?docid=373044.
8. Bennett and Paige, "Why We Need a National School Test."
9. "Thousands of Failing Schools Face Major Overhaul," *CNN.com/Associated Press*, 20 June 2007, www.edu-blogs.com/newssummary.aspx?news=yes&postid=19406 (accessed 11 March 2008).
10. W. James Popham, *America's "Failing" Schools* (New York: Routledge, 2005), 64–65.

11. Jay Mathews, "English, Math Time Up in 'No Child' Era," *Washington Post*, 25 July 2007, www.washingtonpost.com/wp-dyn/content/article/2007/07/24/AR2007072402312.html.

12. Popham, *America's "Failing" Schools*, 64–65.

13. Popham, *America's "Failing" Schools*, 76.

14. Debra Viadero, "Study: Low, High Fliers Gain Less under NCLB," *Education Week*, 1 August 2007, 7.

15. Amit R. Paley, "'No Child' Target Is Called out of Reach," *Washington Post*, 14 March 2007.

16. Paley, "'No Child' Target Is Called out of Reach."

17. Gary Orfield, "No Child Left Behind?" *HGSE News*, 1 September 2002, www.gse.harvard.edu/news/features/orfield09012002.html.

18. David Miller Sadker, Myra Pollack Sadker, and Karen R. Zittleman, *Teachers, Schools, and Society* (Boston: McGraw-Hill, 2008), 232.

19. John Merrow, " Teachers Grapple with Attaining Education Law's Goals," transcript of *NewsHour*, 16 August 2007, PBS Online, www.pbs.org/newshour/bb/education/july-dec07/nclb_08-16.html.

20. Peter W. D. Wright, Pamela Darr Wright, and Suzanne Whitney Heath, *No Child Left Behind* (Hartfield, Va.: Harbor House Law Press, 2006), 6.

21. Wright, Wright, and Heath, *No Child Left Behind*, 38.

II

THE PRESENT

5

HOW ARE WE DOING IN READING? (LANGUAGE ARTS)

For educators, language arts includes more than just the reading skills of students. When one thinks about reading, it usually brings to mind the ability of students to decode and identify words, as well as their skill in comprehending what they are reading. In recent years, schools have frequently used the term "language arts" instead in developing curricula and tests. "Language arts" is a broader term in that it not only includes reading skills and a student's ability to write effectively, but also a student's speaking and listening skills. Some critics of No Child Left Behind have suggested that in emphasizing reading and writing, the law gives too little emphasis to students' ability to communicate orally and to their listening skills. In any case, these two skills are more difficult to assess on a written test.

There is little question that No Child Left Behind places perhaps its greatest emphasis on the goal of improving the reading skills of students in the United States. This is not surprising, given the fact that success in almost every other subject is dependent on children's ability to understand their textbooks and other written materials. To achieve this objective, the law provides a multifaceted approach to ensure that our students become better readers.

The legislation first of all requires that each state develop specific learning standards for reading or the language arts. Second, the law mandates that the states develop appropriate examinations to test these standards. In the area of reading, these tests must be given in grades three through eight. The results of the tests must be reported to the citizens of every school district. A school failing to meet what the law labels as adequate yearly progress faces an escalating number of possible remedial actions. These include a requirement to provide tutoring for children experiencing difficulty. Such tutoring programs must be financed by the district and can include, upon the request of the parents, programs provided by private or even religious agencies.

If such intervention does not effectively raise the test scores, a school, as noted earlier, could be forced to restructure its curriculum or even dismiss administrators and teachers. Supporters of the law obviously believe that such sanctions will motivate school officials to do what is necessary to increase the academic achievement of all students.

Curriculum standards, high-stakes testing, and accountability are not the only aspects of the law designed to improve the reading skills of American students. Another section of the law insists that only "scientifically validated" reading programs should be used in our schools.

To establish appropriate curriculums, districts are eligible to receive specific grants in reading education. The most well-known initiative is the Reading First program. Funds are also available for inservice programs in the area of reading for teachers and administrators.

In addition, No Child Left Behind includes a component titled "Early Reading First," which establishes the possibility of preschool reading programs for three- and four-year-olds. With early intervention, the law attempts to make sure that children are well prepared to begin formal reading training in kindergarten. Money is also available for summer reading programs and special library initiatives. Specific funds sources have been established to help at-risk groups of students, including children of migrant workers and neglected and delinquent children. Other groups that have been singled out include children with limited English proficiency, Hawaiian and Alaskan students, Native American children, and children who are homeless. The legislation also recognizes that schools should be using technology as a way to boost reading scores.[1]

With so many varied aspects of the law aimed at improving the reading skills of the nation's children, it would not be unreasonable to expect that during the last five years there would have been sufficient evidence to allow a neutral observer to judge the effect of No Child Left Behind on reading. Prior to attempting such an analysis, it must be remembered that the legislation allowed individual states a significant degree of independence in developing their own curriculums, tests, and methods used to determine what could be considered acceptable progress. Considering this very significant limiting factor, one can still seek to analyze the information that is available. Perhaps the best way to begin this process is by considering the arguments of those who believe that the law is making a positive difference.

One would expect President Bush and other representatives of his administration to continue to highlight any progress made in test scores since the passage of the No Child Left Behind law. This is especially true since the legislation is likely to be considered one of the most important accomplishments of the Bush presidency. Perhaps more than any law passed by Congress thus far in the twenty-first century, No Child Left Behind, at least its name, is known by most American voters. As early as September 2004, Secretary of Education Rod Paige was trumpeting the success of the law. He was quoted as saying, "I am pleased to report that the law is making a positive difference in millions of lives. . . . There is clear evidence of success, noticeable patterns of change, and upbeat reports all across the nation from a variety of sources. Simply stated: the law is working."[2]

Prior to the presidential election in 2004, there was other evidence of progress being made. The Education Trust, a Washington-based research group, reported that reading scores had improved among fourth and fifth graders in fifteen of twenty-three states.[3] Margaret Spellings, Rod Paige's replacement as secretary of education, has also become a vocal supporter of the law. In a major report published by the Education Department in 2007, the following statistics are highlighted in an introductory section titled "No Child Left Behind Is Working":

In the 1990s, reading remained stagnant for fourth-graders nationwide. . . . More reading progress has been made by nine-year-olds in five years (1999–2004) than in the previous twenty-eight years combined; . . . Achievement gaps in reading . . . between African-American and Hispanic nine-year-olds and their white peers have fallen to an all-time low.[4]

President Bush has also frequently pointed to the successes being made in the area of reading education. Speaking at a school in Washington, D.C., he claimed "good progress" under the law. Like Secretary Spellings, he highlighted the fact that "in reading, nine-year-olds have made larger gains in the past five years than at any point in the previous twenty-eight years."[5] Another report released by the federal government in 2007 highlights the same statistic concerning nine-year-olds, but also includes some additional accomplishments. It points out that this age group of African-American and Hispanic students accomplished an all-time high in their reading scores.[6]

It is not only the federal government that has released information concerning improvements in reading scores. In the spring of 2006, the Council of the Great City Schools was already claiming that on state-sponsored tests, because of No Child Left Behind, children in sixty-one urban school districts from thirty-seven states were showing improvement in their reading scores. This study also noted that the greatest improvements were at the fourth-grade level.[7] Another research project conducted by the Center on Education Policy concluded that "the nation's students have performed significantly better on state reading . . . tests since President Bush signed his landmark education initiative into law five years ago." The same report "concluded that the achievement gap between black and white students is shrinking in many states and that the pace of student gains increased after the law was enacted."[8]

Since No Child Left Behind requires that each state develop its own test, one must look separately at the results for each individual state. Scanning newspapers throughout the country, it is possible to find examples of areas where reading scores have improved. An example would be a newspaper account published in North Carolina that claims that 71.2 percent of the state's students met or exceeded academic expectations on state exams in the 2006–2007 school year. This was compared to 54.3 percent during the prior year.[9] A similar story appeared in the *Los Angeles Times* with the headline "Student Test Scores Up Since 2002." This article states that in nine of thirteen states, "gains were faster after No Child Left Behind." It also notes that "there is more evidence of achievement gaps between groups of students narrowing since 2002 than with gaps widening."[10]

More influential than individual state reading test results was a story broadcast on ABC News. Network reporters spent months investigating the effect of the No Child Left Behind law. They found "something critics may be surprised to learn—in a lot of places, it's working." The program reported to the nation that "state and national numbers on reading and math show some progress." As a result, the commentator gave an "A-" to the law for meeting its major goal of raising test scores to meet specific educational standards.[11]

It should be noted that in each of the articles that have been quoted, there were qualifying statements that questioned either the statistics used or whether the law was indeed a major factor in raising the scores. This ambivalence can be seen in a June 2007 article in *Education Week*. The main headline is "State Tests Show Gains Since NCLB," but underneath it is the sub-headline "Report Cautions Against Crediting Education Law." The article begins with the following statement: "Scores on state tests have increased consistently and significantly in the five years since the No Child Left Behind Act became law, and there's some evidence that gains that started in the 1990s accelerated after the law's enactment, a new report concludes." But the author, David J. Hoff, adds: "These findings should be treated very cautiously . . . especially trying to link this to something as amorphous as NCLB."[12]

While press coverage has included stories highlighting gains in reading scores since the passage of No Child Left Behind, there are at least as many stories that would cause people to question that there has been progress. One of the most important criticisms comes from those who question the tests developed by states to measure students' progress in reading. They are critical of changing standards that may be lowering academic expectations. If a state lowers its expectations, it would certainly follow that it would lead to higher scores. No Child Left Behind mandates that students be "proficient" in the area of reading. It is the state bureaucracy that determines the level a student must reach to be considered proficient. An article published in *Education Week* charges that "many of the states that claim to have large shares of their students reaching proficiency in reading and mathematics under the No Child Left Behind Act have set less stringent standards for meeting that threshold than lower-performing states."[13]

In support of this assertion, the author compares the results on the state reading test to those of a national examination administered by the National Assessment of Educational Progress (NAEP). This test, which is given to sample students in every state, has been called "The Nation's Report Card." An agency known as the National Center for Education Statistics "compares where states set minimum scores for determining whether students are proficient, under the mandates of the No Child Left Behind Act, against the bar set by NAEP on the fourth and eighth grade reading and math scores." This comparison "found that state tests varied greatly in judging students as proficient—between 60 and 80 points—when placed on the NAEP 500-point scale." The difference was especially evident in the fourth-grade scores, which the federal government was citing as a great success.[14]

In the prestigious education journal *Phi Delta Kappan*, Anne C. Lewis looks at the results of the study noted above and concludes that "reading scores were flat" and that No Child Left Behind, as a "silver bullet" for education, "is pretty much a dud." For her, the report of the National Center for Education Statistics showed that "students in some states are being held accountable for much higher levels of performance than students in other states. And no state has made much progress as revealed in the NAEP scores."[15]

Another article in the August 2007 issue of *Education Week* carried the headline "12-State Study Finds Falloff in Testing Gains After NCLB." The study discussed in this article was published in the July issue of *Education Researcher*, which is a peer-reviewed journal of the Washington-based American Education Research Association. The group concluded that, at least in the twelve states that were studied,

"since the enactment of the No Child Left Behind Law, test-score improvement among fourth graders in twelve states has fallen off in
reading." This author also states that "after NCLB, earlier progress
made by the states actually petered out." In addition, the article
claims that "black and Latino students' fourth grade reading proficiency has not appreciably narrowed the gap with white students'
scores under the NCLB law."[16]

The Public Broadcasting System (PBS) also pointed to the manipulation of tests in order to show progress under No Child Left Behind.
Veteran education writer and television correspondent John Merrow
broadcast a three-part analysis of the law in July 2007. The program
highlighted the difference between the reported state results and
those on the NAEP. In an interview with education expert Kevin
Carey, the following information was highlighted: Fourth graders in
the state of Mississippi have the highest passing rate in the nation on
their state test. On the federal test, these same students have the second lowest passing rate in the country. In the states of Tennessee, Oklahoma, and Colorado, approximately 90 percent of students showed
proficiency in their state test, but less than 40 percent passed the federal examination. In response to being questioned about these results,
Secretary Spellings said, "I'm confident that the people of [those]
state[s] will look at that information and will act on that."[17]

Even more damning is the claim that reading scores actually improved more in the years between the mid-1990s and 2002 than they
have over the years since No Child Left Behind was passed.[18] While a
number of states and cities did report progress in reading scores as a result of No Child Left Behind, others have seen less positive results. The
Washington Post, in August 2007, carried the headline, "More Md. Elementary, Middle Schools Fall Short of 'No Child' Goals."[19] On the same
day, the *San Diego Union-Tribune* published a story that suggests that, at
least in its own city, a wide achievement gap continues between Asian-
American and white students and black and Latino students. The story
notes that "the disparity in achievement is stark" and that the problem is
true throughout California. In the area of "English/language arts, only 30
percent of black students and 29 percent of Latino students scored proficient or better. In contrast, 62 percent of white students and 66 percent
of Asian students scored proficient or better."[20] The *Los Angeles Times*

carried a similar story about the difference in scores. The matter has come to the attention of the Hispanic community, as they have considered results of the national testing. The problem of the English language learner is not unique to California. The Pew Hispanic Center reported that "nearly three quarters [of English language learners] (73 percent) scored below basic in reading."[21]

As if there wasn't enough bad news in the summer of 2007, a headline in the *Wall Street Journal* was certainly likely to catch the attention of those who were unsure about the progress of our public education system. The story reported that "the reading SAT scores had fallen to the lowest level since 1999."[22] A knowledgeable reader, however, might be able to figure out that the Scholastic Achievement Test (SAT) scores of the class of 2007 should not have been expected to be affected by the No Child Left Behind Act. The fact is that one of the major reasons for the lower scores is that more and more students take the examination each year. It is also true that the No Child Left Behind legislation was focused primarily on the early grades rather than on the high school students who take the SAT examination. Unfortunately, many people associated any bad news about test scores with the law.

Despite the continuing criticism of our public schools and the claims that No Child Left Behind has had little positive effect on the reading skills of our students, certainly it is true that, at least in certain localities, the scores are improving. It is close to impossible to reach definitive conclusions on the effect of the law unless it is determined that the federal government should mandate a specific reading curriculum and national testing. Although there are influential supporters of this approach, it does not appear that this will occur as part of the current reauthorization of the law.

About the tests now used to evaluate students' progress in reading, a number of educational assessment authorities agree with W. James Popham when he argues that the current standards-based tests are too narrow. They also concur that standardized tests, such as the California Achievement Test and the Iowa Test of Basic Skills, "were never intended to evaluate schools, and they just can't do it properly."[23] At the same time, it appears that because teachers are too often gearing their teaching to whatever test their state adopts, they are unable to deal with all of the standards identified in the language arts curriculum. Some of those standards, such as listening and speaking skills, would be difficult to measure on any written test. According to Popham, "teachers, who are under great pressure to boost their students' scores on high-stakes tests, are thus forced to play a guessing game regarding which content standards will be assessed on a given year's standards-based tests."[24] Many educators also agree that one test at the end of the year should not be used to judge a school's success or failure in teaching reading.

Although it is unlikely that anyone would question the importance of reading skills for any student's comprehensive education, there are those who believe that we are emphasizing reading to the point that schools are neglecting other essential areas of the curriculum. In an article in *Phi Delta Kappan* magazine, Jack Jennings and Diane Starkrentner report that:

> 71 percent of districts are reducing time spent in other subjects in elementary school—at least to some degree. The subject most affected is social studies, while physical education is least affected. In addition, 60 percent of districts require a specific amount of time for reading in elementary schools. Ninety-seven percent of high-poverty districts have this requirement, compared to 55 percent–59 percent of districts with lower levels of poverty.[25]

On a more positive note, the same authors suggest that because of the provisions of No Child Left Behind, schools are being forced to pay more attention to the needs of those students who have historically lagged behind on reading test scores. The law makes provisions for tutoring opportunities for such students. It is also true that administrators and teachers are spending more time considering the best possible instructional methods and are seeking to ensure that the methods and materials they are using are aligned with the state curriculum standards. They are being assisted in this task by taking time to analyze the test data that are now available to them. In addition, they are, more than ever, using "research to inform their decisions about improvement strategies."[26] Finally, schools are engaged in additional professional development for their teachers and administrators as they seek to learn about the most effective ways to teach students to learn to read.

If one were to ask a large sample of educational and political leaders for their opinion on how our schools are doing, the range of answers would vary greatly. There are those who claim that the law has been a disaster for our schools. This group would likely include, among others, those who support the whole-language method of teaching reading. This method, which was so popular in the last years of the twentieth century, called for the use of excellent children's literature as the basis for lessons, as opposed to the traditional Basal readers and workbooks. This approach deemphasizes phonics as the sole method for helping students to recognize new words. Instead, whole-language teachers teach students to use context clues to help them to identify an unknown word. This literature-based approach had students' weekly spelling words and writing assignments taken from the literature they were reading rather than using workbooks. No Child Left Behind appears to emphasize a more traditional approach to reading instruction.

On the other hand, while there are those who wish to oppose any reauthorization of the law, it would seem that a majority agrees that with certain appropriate changes, the nation could continue to follow the directions outlined in the original legislation. There will undoubtedly be, in the area of reading, some changes.

Even though reading remains perhaps the primary concern of both educators and politicians, improving the math skills of our nation's students is an objective that is very close behind.

NOTES

1. Peter W. D. Wright, Pamela Darr Wright, and Suzanne Whitney Heath, *No Child Left Behind* (Hartfield, Va.: Harbor House Law Press, 2004), 25–39.

2. Erik W. Robelen, "Paige: It's Not Too Early to Call School Law a Success," *Education Week*, 6 October 2004, www.edweek.org/ew/articles/2004/10/06/06Paige.h24.html.

3. Debra Viadero, "Report: States See Test-Score Gains," *Education Week*, 20 October 2004, www.edweek.org/ew/articles/2004/10/20/08EdTrust.h24.html.

4. Margaret Spellings, *No Child Left Behind, Building on Results: A Blueprint for Strengthening the No Child Left Behind Act* (Washington, D.C.: U.S. Department of Education, January 2007), 2.

5. President George Bush, "President Bush Discusses No Child Left Behind," transcript of speech at Woodridge Elementary and Middle Campus, Washington, D.C., 5 October 2006, www.whitehouse.gov/news/releases/2006/10/20061005-6.html (accessed 6 September 2007).

6. U.S. Department of Education, *No Child Left Behind Act Is Working*, December 2006, www.ed.gov/nclb/overview/importance/nclbworking.html.

7. Council of the Great City Schools, "Study Finds Urban School Progress Since No Child Left Behind," 22 March 2004, www.cgcs.org/images/PDF_PReleases/NCLB.pdf (accessed 10 September 2007).

8. Amit R. Paley, "No Child Left Behind Law Aiding Test Scores?" *Seattle Times*, 6 June 2007, http://seattletimes.nwsource.com/html/nationworld/2003736070_nochild06.html.

9. T. Keung Hui, "N.C. Students, Schools Show Improvement," *News & Observer*, 6 September 2007.

10. Howard Blume, "Student Test Scores Up Since 2002," *Los Angeles Times*, 6 June 2007.

11. ABC News, "Report Card: No Child Left Behind," 29 May 2007, www.abcnews.go.com/GMA/Politics/Story?id=3221230.

12. David J. Hoff, "State Tests Show Gains Since NCLB," *Education Week*, 6 June 2007, 1.

13. Sean Cavanagh, "State Tests, NAEP Often a Mismatch," *Education Week*, 7 June 2007, www.edweek.org/ew/articles/2007/06/13/41proficient.h26.html.

14. Cavanagh, "State Tests."

15. Anne C. Lewis, "An Ammunition Dump," *Phi Delta Kappan*, December 2005, 260.

16. Scott J. Cech, "12-State Study Finds Falloff in Testing Gains After NCLB," *Education Week*, 1 August 2007, 9.

17. "School Districts Find Loopholes in No Child Left Behind Law," transcript of *NewsHour*, 14 August 2007, PBS Online, www.pbs.org/newshour/bb/education/july-dec07/nclb_08-14.html.

18. American Educational Research Association, "Test Scores Slow under No Child Left Behind Reforms, Gauged by States/Federal Assessment," 30

July 2007, www.eurekalert.org/pub_releases/2007-07/aera-tss073007.php (accessed 8 August 2007).

19. Daniel de Vise, "More Md. Elementary, Middle Schools Fall Short of 'No Child' Goals," *Washington Post*, 16 August 2007, www.washingtonpost.com/wp-dyn/content/article/2007/08/15/AR2007081501235.html.

20. Bruce Lieberman, "A Wide Achievement Gap," *San Diego Union-Tribune*, www.signonsandiego.com/uniontrib/20070816/news_lm16star.html.

21. Rick Fry, "How Far Behind in Math and Reading Are English Language Learners?" Pew Hispanic Center, 6 June 2007, http://pewhispanic.org/reports/report.php?ReportID=76.

22. Anne Marie Chaker, "Class of 2007 Logs Slide in SAT Scores," *Wall Street Journal*, 28 August 2007, online.wsj.com/article/SB118830451239510896.html.

23. W. James Popham, *America's "Failing" Schools* (New York: Routledge, 2005), 67.

24. Popham, *America's "Failing" Schools*, 79.

25. Jack Jennings and Diane Starkrentner, "Ten Big Effects of the No Child Left Behind Act on Public Schools," *Phi Delta Kappan*, October 2006, 110–11.

26. Jennings and Starkrentner, "Big Ten Effects," 111.

6

WHAT IS HAPPENING IN MATH?

During the past quarter century, the importance of improving math education in the United States has received a great deal of attention. Beginning with the *Nation at Risk* report in 1983, the business and scientific communities especially have pushed to raise the mathematical literacy of our students. This well-publicized report noted that between 1963 and 1980, the average mathematics scores on the College Board's Scholastic Aptitude Tests (SAT) had dropped nearly forty points.[1] It also pointed out that our students spend less time on mathematics in high school than students in other advanced nations.[2] In a section of the report called "The New Basics," the authors called for requiring three years of high-school math rather than one, which was then the requirement in thirty-five states.[3]

In the final decade of the twentieth century, there was additional public pressure for improving math education. The need was highlighted in a best-selling book titled *The World Is Flat*, written by *New York Times* columnist Thomas L. Friedman. For Friedman, our nation's schools and colleges were failing dismally in preparing enough scientists and engineers to allow the United States to remain competitive with nations like China and India. Like earlier critics, he emphasized that our students' test scores are "hovering near the bottom in international tests related to math."[4]

Making our nation competitive in the world economy was also an important factor in giving to mathematics special attention in the No Child Left Behind legislation. In a report of the Department of Education titled *Answering the Challenge of a Changing World*, Secretary of Education Margaret Spellings is quoted as saying, "We must improve the way we teach math in our elementary schools. It's not just about helping younger students develop strong arithmetic skills; it's about planting the seeds of higher-order thinking for later in life."[5] This document outlines the components of President Bush's 2007 "American Competitiveness Initiative" in the field of mathematics:

National Mathematics Panel ($10 million): Modeled after the influential National Reading Panel, the National Math Panel would convene experts to empirically evaluate the effectiveness of various approaches to teaching math, creating a research base to improve instructional methods for teachers. It would lay the groundwork for the Math Now program for grades K–7 to prepare every student to take and pass algebra.

Math Now for Elementary School Students ($125 million): Like the successful and popular Reading First program, Math Now for Elementary School Students would promote promising, research-based practices in mathematics instruction and prepare students for more rigorous math course work in middle and high school.

Math Now for Middle School Students ($125 million): Similar to the current Striving Readers Initiative, Math Now for Middle School Students would diagnose students' deficiencies in math proficiency and provide intensive and systematic instruction to enable them to take and pass algebra.

Advanced Placement-International Baccalaureate (AP-IB) Incentive Program ($122 million—$90 million over 2006 levels): The AP-IB Incentive Program would train 70,000 additional teachers to lead AP-IB math, science, and critical-need language courses over the next five years. It would increase the number of students taking AP-IB tests to 1.5 million by 2012, tripling the number of passing test-takers to approximately 700,000 while giving them the opportunity to earn college credit.[6]

The added emphasis on math in our schools can also be seen in a recently published study showing that on average, the number of minutes per week spent on math increased by 37 percent.[7] Strangely enough, even though this is happening, parents and students do not necessarily believe that it is important. In one survey of 2,600 students and parents, it was found that "only 25 percent of the parents think their children should be studying more math . . . and 70 percent think things 'are fine as they are now.'" Seventy-two percent of the students believe that they should not be forced to take advanced math courses.[8]

Even though parents and students might not support the trend, there is little question that teachers are spending more time in school teaching math. Whether or not this new emphasis is making a difference is open to question. It is true that even by 2004, individual states were claiming success in raising their test scores. In a press release by the New York State Education Department, it was reported that math test scores in both 2003 and 2004 had improved in both the elementary and middle schools of the state. The commissioner of education, Richard Mills, claimed in the release that "higher standards, with support to achieve them and tests to measure them, have helped many children immensely. The progress so far should give us reason to hope and press on." While the state education bureaucracy was reporting these improved test scores, it is also true that they gave no credit for the improved scores to the No Child Left Behind law.[9]

As with the improved test scores in reading, the reports that highlighted better math results in various states did not usually claim that they were a result of the No Child Left Behind law. On the other hand, it seems significant that when comparing the improvement between reading test scores and math test scores, the evidence seems to point that we are doing better in mathematics. For example, in one major study reported in *Education Week*, which was based on three years of data, thirty-seven of the forty-one states studied "reported increases of at least 1 percentage point per year in the proportion of students scoring at the proficient level or above" in elementary school mathematics. In the field of reading, only twenty-nine states showed such gains.[10]

Even though it appeared early on that there was progress in mathematics by 2005, the *Washington Post* reported that improvement was "slower than in previous years." Still, during the same time period, Secretary Spellings chose to focus on "a narrowing of the achievement gap between white and minority students." The *Post* article, like many others, illustrated that progress was greater in math than in reading.[11] For example, *Time* magazine, in September 2007, concluded that "math scores are creeping up, but reading scores are flat."[12]

The same month, the *New York Times* carried the headline "Math Scores Rise, But Reading Is Mixed." According to the article, "the average score for fourth graders is at its highest level in seventeen years, and the percentage of fourth graders scoring at or above proficiency rose to 39 percent this year." The eighth-grade students' math performance also improved, but not as quickly as the elementary students. Unfortunately, the gains were very uneven, with some states, including Massachusetts and New Jersey, improving dramatically, while the eighth graders in New York state actually showed a decline.[13]

Despite more positive math results, the rate of improvement is far below what is demanded by the No Child Left Behind law. Using the nationally accepted test produced by the National Assessment of Education Progress, it would require fourth graders "to have an annual improvement rate 3.9 times faster than the rate of increase between 1996 and 2003. For eighth-grade mathematics, the rate of improvement would need to be 7.5 times faster. Such rapid acceleration of math achievement is unrealistic."[14]

To increase the progress being made in raising scores in mathematics, a number of initiatives are underway. The federal government has initiated programs that allow differential pay for mathematics teachers, signing bonuses, and financial incentive to hire "highly qualified teachers" in "high-needs subjects" such as math.[15] These extras are available primarily in high poverty schools. Scholarships are also being offered to well-qualified applicants to teacher education programs who are preparing to teach mathematics. As part of the original legislation, a mathematics and science partnership program was also established. This plan provides money to the states and other educational organizations to participate in programs that:

Improve and upgrade the status and stature of mathematics and science teaching by encouraging IHEs [institutions of higher education] to improve mathematics and science teacher education;

Focus on the education of mathematics and science teachers as a career-long process;

Bring mathematics and science teachers together with scientists, mathematicians, and engineers to improve their teaching skills; and

Develop more rigorous mathematics and science curricula that are aligned with state and local academic achievement standards expected for postsecondary study in engineering, mathematics, and science.[16]

Another promising program is sponsored by the National Science Foundation, which is "an independent federal agency that supports fundamental research and education across all fields of science and engineering." It has an annual budget of $5.92 billion and the funds are distributed to groups in all fifty states, representing over 1,700 universities and institutions. The agency reported in 2007 that "students' performance on annual math and science assessments improved in almost every age group when their schools were involved in their program that partners K–12 teachers with their colleagues in higher education."[17]

There are others who believe that the most effective way to boost achievement in mathematics is to create "a common, coherent, and challenging curriculum" for all students in the United States. In making the argument for a national curriculum, William H. Schmidt argues that those countries having the highest scores on international tests do use a national curriculum. In these countries, the students at each grade level have a prescribed curriculum that is rigorous and well articulated. To him, at least, "our teachers deserve it; our students need it; the laudable vision of NCLB demands it."[18]

While there will continue to be ongoing arguments concerning a national curriculum and national tests, educators also remain engaged in a debate concerning not only what should be taught, but also how it should be taught. During the last century, schools in the United States have experimented with the "new math," mastery learning, "hands-on math," and Madeline Hunter's *Elements of Instruction*. The most basic conflict has actually been going on for over a century.

It is what David J. Ferrero has called the "hundred years' war" between progressive and traditional educators. For him:

> Progressives incline toward pedagogical approaches that start with student interest and emphasize hands-on engagement with the physical and social environments, whereas traditionalists tend to start with pre-existing canons of inquiry and knowledge and emphasize ideas and concepts mediated through words and symbols.[19]

A more complete contrast between the two approaches can be seen in table 6.1.

John Dewey, the most well known of the progressive educators, believes that

> the teacher is not in school to impose certain ideas or to form certain habits in the child, but is there as a member of the community to select the influences which shall affect the child and to assist him in properly responding to these influences. . . . Examinations are of use only so far as they test the child's fitness for social life and reveal the place in which he can be of most service and where he can receive most help.[20]

A current application of the progressive approach can be seen in a method that has been labeled "Teaching Mathematics Thematically."

Table 6.1. Traditional Philosophy versus Contemporary Progressivism

Traditional Philosophy	Contemporary Progressivism
Textbooks and workbooks dominate; teaching and learning largely contained to classroom.	Varied instructional materials; teaching and learning include community resources.
Whole-group learning; fixed schedules; uniform time periods.	Whole, small, and individualized groups; flexible schedules; adjustable time periods.
Emphasis on uniformity of classroom experiences and instructional situations.	Emphasis on variability of classroom experiences and instructional situations.
Curriculum is prescribed; little room for electives.	Mix of liberal arts, practical, and vocational subjects.
Excellence and high standards; special consideration for high achievers.	Equality and flexible standards; special consideration for low achievers.

Educators supporting this method emphasize "the use of applications of mathematics around a central theme whereas teaching in topics predominantly emphasizes mathematics content." One author uses the example of a theme based on sports. Such a unit would include such topics as "percentages, measurement, statistics or algebra, and in all these areas sport-related applications of mathematics will be emphasized."[21]

The conflict in math education is between traditional educators who emphasize memorization and drills and the progressive educators who oppose such an emphasis on rote learning and instead support opportunities for students to deal with practical problems in which they would learn by doing. Some progressive educators are very concerned about teaching students how to understand the theory of mathematics and want to put less emphasis on just teaching how to do mathematics. In the area of math education especially, we must somehow get past this conflict between the traditionalists and the progressives. Students do have to memorize basic facts and formulas, but classes can also become engaged in practical problem-solving activities. Progressives do have trouble with the emphasis on testing and "teaching to the test" that seems to be a by-product of No Child Left Behind. One way to minimize this concern is to devise assessments, including test questions, that offer opportunities for students to use their math skills to solve real problems. In dealing with the difference between educators on how to teach math, as well as how to teach any subject, our educational community might benefit from considering the words of John Dewey, who ended his book *Experience and Education* with this thought:

> The fundamental issue is not of new versus old education nor of progressive against traditional education but a question of what anything whatever must be to be worthy of the name education. I am not, I hope and believe, in favor of any ends or any methods simply because the name progressive may be applied to them. . . . What we want and need is education pure and simple, and we shall make sure and faster progress when we devote ourselves to finding out just what education is and what conditions have to be satisfied in order that education may be a reality and not a name or a slogan.[22]

As with reading, it is possible that progressive and traditional educators can find some agreement. Both accept the goal of increasing achievement in these crucial areas.

Even if this agreement does occur, however, there is a growing concern that the additional focus placed on both reading and math by No Child Left Behind is having an adverse impact on other areas of the curriculum.

NOTES

1. U.S. Department of Education, the National Commission on Excellence in Education, "Introduction," *A Nation at Risk: The Imperative for Educational Reform* (Washington, D.C., April 1983), 2–3.

2. U.S. Department of Education, "Findings," *A Nation at Risk*, 2.

3. U.S. Department of Education, "Recommendations," *A Nation at Risk*, 1.

4. Thomas L. Friedman, *The World Is Flat* (New York: Farrar, Straus and Giroux, 2005), 273.

5. U.S. Department of Education, *Answering the Challenge of a Changing World: Strengthening Education for the 21st Century* (Washington, D.C., April 2006), 9.

6. U.S. Department of Education, *Answering the Challenge of a Changing World*, 13–14.

7. Jay Mathews, "English, Math Time Up in 'No Child' Era," *Washington Post*, 25 July 2007, www.washingtonpost.com/wp-dyn/content/article/2007/07/24/AR2007072402312.html.

8. Michelle R. Davis, "Parents, Students Feel Less Urgency for Math, Science Upgrades," *Education Week*, 19 September 2007, www.edweek.org/ew/articles/2007/09/19/05stempoll_web.h27.html.

9. The New York State Education Department, "Elementary and Middle School Math Achievement Improve in 2004, Show Major Gains Since Higher Standards and Tests Began in 1999," 6 October 2004, www.emsc.nysed.gov/deputy/Documents/press-release-10-6-math.htm (accessed 14 September 2007).

10. David J. Hoff, "State Tests Show Gains Since NCLB," *Education Week*, 5 June 2007, www.edweek.org/ew/articles/2007/06/06/39cep.h26.html.

11. Lois Romano, "Test Scores Move Little in Math, Reading," *Washington Post*, 20 October 2005, www.washingtonpost.com/wp-dyn/content/article/2005/10/19/AR2005101900708.html.

12. Claudia Wallis and Sonja Steptoe, "How to Fix No Child Left Behind," *Time*, 24 May 2007, www.time.com/time/printout/0,8816,1625192,00.html.

13. Sam Dillon, "Math Scores Rise, But Reading Is Mixed," *New York Times*, 26 September 2007.

14. Robert L. Linn, *Fixing the NCLB Accountability System*, CRESST Policy Brief #8 (Los Angeles: National Center for Research on Evaluation, Standards, and Student Testing, Summer 2005), 2.

15. U.S. Department of Education, *Recognizing and Rewarding Our Best Teachers*, June 2007, www.ed.gov/nclb/methods/teachers/incentivefund.html (accessed 18 April 2008).

16. U.S. Department of Education, *Mathematics and Science Partnerships*, 13 October 2006, www.ed.gov/programs/mathsci/index.html (accessed 11 September 2007).

17. National Science Foundation, "Student Results Show Benefits of Math and Science Partnerships," 18 July 2007, www.nsf.gov/news/news_summ.jsp?cntn_id=109725 (accessed 9 August 2007).

18. William H. Schmidt, "A Vision for Mathematics," *Educational Leadership*, February 2004, 1, 11.

19. David J. Ferrero, "Pathways to Reform: Start with Values," *Educational Leadership* 62, no. 5 (February 2005): 10.

20. John Dewey, "My Pedagogic Creed," *School Journal* 54, No. 3 (January 16, 1897): 77–80. Also available in the Informal Education Archives at www.infed.org/archives/e-texts/e-dew-pc.htm.

21. Boris Handal and Janette Bobis, "Teaching Mathematics Thematically: Teachers' Perspectives," *Mathematics Education Research Journal* 16, no. 1 (2004): 1.

22. L. Glen Smith and Joan K. Smith, *Lives in Education* (New York: St. Martin's Press, 1994), 294.

⑦

THE OTHER SUBJECTS

In previous chapters, it has been noted that the mandatory testing in grades three through eight in the areas of reading and math has caused many schools to increase the time spent teaching these subjects. Since most schools have not changed the total number of hours available for instruction, it is inevitable that less time is being spent on other subjects. One study conducted in 349 school districts found that "44 percent of school districts nationwide have made deep cuts in social studies, science, art and music lessons in elementary grades and have even slashed lunch time."[1] The *New York Times* reported on another study, which had an even more dramatic finding. The article included a description of a survey conducted by the Center on Education Policy, which found that "since the passage of the federal law, 71 percent of the nation's 15,000 school districts had reduced the hours of instructional time spent on history, music and other subjects to open more time for reading and math."[2]

Advocates for academic areas other than reading and math have become very vocal in their criticisms of what they see as a narrowing of the curriculum. The subject area that is least likely to be affected in the near future is science. This was not true in elementary schools during the first several years after the passage of the law. There may have been less time spent in science then because it was not a subject that was tested. Beginning during the 2007–2008 school year, however, No Child Left Behind mandates that all students be tested at least three times in science during their years in school. The law states that schools must "measure the proficiency of all students in science and that tests must be administered not less than one time" in grades three through five, six through nine, and ten through twelve.[3]

For students in grades three through eight, this means that they will only be tested twice in science, while they will take language arts and math tests in each grade, but, unlike in the other two basic subjects, students must also be tested during their high-school years in science. It is also true that improving science education, as with mathematics, is a popular cause among political and business leaders. One can expect that the progress on science test scores will be carefully monitored. Although in the future it is likely that even more time will be spent on science in our classrooms, just as in mathematics, educators will continue to differ on the best way to teach the subject.

It has been suggested that mandatory science tests could "force schools to consider cutting back on some of the in-class experiments many teachers value." With science, the debate is between those who favor the use of laboratory experiments that are built around "discovery learning" and those who favor direct instruction, which can "easily regress into lecture-style teaching, heavy on rote recitation of scientific facts and memorization."[4] After some debate, the state of California has concluded that in science classes "at least 20 percent to 25 percent of K-8 class time be devoted to hands-on activities, as long as those experiments are connected to state standards."[5] However the schools choose to divide their time between laboratories and direct instruction, it seems that science will remain a prominent part of our public-school curriculum.

The same cannot be said about social studies. Here the level of concern has been expressed by a spokesman of the National Council for Social Studies, who is quoted as saying, "The worst thing that has ever happened to social studies has been the No Child Left Behind law."[6] Historian David McCullough testified to a committee of the United States Senate that because of No Child Left Behind, "history is being put on the back burner or taken off the stove all together in many or most schools, in favor of math and reading."[7]

When we consider the fact that the social studies curriculum is made up not only of history, but also economics, geography, and civics or political science, it is evident that cutting back on such a subject can indeed have a major effect on the education of our children. This is especially true as it relates to preparing them to be productive citizens. Social studies is likely to remain a required subject in middle schools and high schools, with the reduction in instructional time taking place at the elementary level. One approach that might be helpful is to try to combine reading and writing instruction with social studies. This concept is sometimes referred to as "reading in the content areas." The idea is that both reading and writing assignments could be taken from social studies books that students are assigned to read. Such assignments are often more interesting to students than those that are taken from reading textbooks and workbooks.

Another possible solution is to create mandatory testing in the area of social studies. Of course if we begin to add more tests, it is difficult to know where to stop. It would certainly be possible to develop mandatory tests in music, art, and foreign languages. Like social studies educators, those involved in these other subjects are also concerned about the impact of No Child Left Behind on their academic areas. David Conrad has written in the *Phi Kappa Phi Forum* that "music teachers are normally an optimistic and progressive group. Over the past few years, however, I have heard more and more of my public school music colleagues say that they feel worn-out and frustrated by recent developments affecting American music education." Title V of No Child Left Behind does provide funds for innovative programs in the arts. In addition, they are included in the definition of core subjects, but they are certainly not featured in the bill.[8]

The time crunch in the elementary school can affect not only general music classes but also performing groups. The *American Teacher*, a publication of the American Federation of Teachers, has shown its concern over music programs in a recent issue, reporting that some schools that once allowed time during the school day for the rehearsals of band, orchestra, and chorus have now required that the groups practice either before or after school. Release time for music lessons might also be curtailed to ensure students do not miss reading and math instruction. The magazine quotes a music teacher who "spoke of how instruments in her classroom now gather dust because the school has prioritized NCLB test-prep instruction over music."[9]

As criticism over decisions to reduce time spent on the arts grew, Secretary of Education Paige wrote a letter to all school superintendents stating that "the arts, perhaps more than any other subject, help students to understand themselves and others, whether they lived in the past or are living in the present." He went on to claim that "districts have enough flexibility under the law to include arts in their curriculum" and the letter "enumerated places where they could ask for discretionary federal money for arts programming."[10] The letter has apparently done little to reverse the pattern of stealing time from music education. Still, the arts do have their champions.

Presidential candidate Mike Huckabee, for example, wrote in the *New York Times*:

> Across the nation, schools are trimming back financing for music and the arts in the name of 'efficiency' and 'core subjects.' This is beyond short-sighted. It's stupid. . . . Numerous studies affirm that a student schooled in music improves his or her SAT and ACT scores in math, foreign language, or creative writing. Creative students are better problem-solvers; that is a trait the business world begs for in its work force.[11]

Reynold Levy, president of the Lincoln Center for the Performing Arts, in a book titled *Letters to the Next President*, also has written about the educational value of the arts. His letter suggests that "today, there is a growing recognition of the positive impact of arts education on student learning across the curriculum. There is a growing appreciation of a renewed emphasis on the arts as being complementary to, rather than competitive with, the back-to-basics movement which stressed language and math literacy."[12]

Funding is also an issue in many districts. Music and art classes can be among the most expensive programs offered in schools. When a district is weighing a string program against hiring remedial reading teachers, one can see why boards of education might consider the music elective to be expendable. Unfortunately, outstanding music programs seem to flourish most often in wealthy suburban districts rather than in rural and urban schools. In his letter to the superintendents, Secretary Paige wrote, "We all know that NCLB provides a disincentive for schools to invest in the arts unless school officials take the time and trouble to investigate how the arts help them meet their reading and math goals."[13]

Despite his cautionary advice, school districts are most likely going to continue to seek educational programs that will have a more immediate effect on their test scores. This could easily mean that a summer music program would be replaced by summer remedial reading classes. A press release by the American Music Conference argues that there is new research that supports a strong correlation between music and other academic subjects. The release notes the following:

> A new study led by Dr. Agnes S. Chan of the Chinese University of Hong Kong, published in July in the journal *Neuropsychology*, found that school-age students who had participated in music scored significantly higher on verbal memory tests than their classmates who had not.
> A 1999 UCLA study showed that students who participated in music programs three times a week scored an average of 40 percent higher in math, reading, history, and geography than those who did not.
> Other research over the last decade has linked music participation with enhanced brain development, higher performance in other academic courses, better socialization, and improved wellness.[14]

Like music teachers, visual arts educators are also concerned about reductions in time for their classes and money being allotted to their programs. Nina Ozlu, the chief counsel for America for the Arts, was quoted in *Education World* as saying that despite statements of support for the arts from two secretaries of education, "the [Bush] administration attempts to zero it out in the budget each year."[15] To justify their programs, art teachers are being urged to do what is necessary to integrate language arts and math activities into their own curriculum. An example is given where a teacher assigns a short story for the students to read and then they are asked to prepare illustrations for that story. Organizations supporting the arts are also urging art teachers to become vocal advocates of their programs.[16]

Along with music and the visual arts, foreign language instruction, especially at the elementary and middle-school level, appears also to be a target for cuts. In the United States, we do less instruction of foreign language in the early grades than almost any country in the world. In most states, students have little or no foreign language experience before high school, or at best the middle-school level. Mary Abbott, director of education for the American Council of Teachers of Foreign Languages, reports that "only about 5 percent of elementary school students are taking a foreign language." The number is higher at the middle-school level, but it appears that school districts could easily decide to reduce or eliminate such instruction in order to substitute additional time for reading and math. At the high-school level, a study by the National K-12 Foreign Language Resource Center found that "22 percent of school districts have eliminated one or more foreign language courses." Abbott goes on to say, "Expecting the rest of the world to learn English is not the way to understand other people. . . . The way to understand other people is by learning their language and culture."[17]

Perhaps even more controversial than the reduction in time being spent on foreign language instruction is the charge that schools are dramatically cutting their physical education programs. This is being done at a time when studies are reporting that a growing number of our nation's children are overweight. Supporters of physical education are arguing that schools should be doing more and not less in the areas of health education and physical education.

A study prepared by the American Heart Association and the National Association for Sport and Physical Education concluded in 2006 that "most states are failing to provide students with adequate physical education requirements." They also noted that the percentage of students who have a daily physical education class dropped fourteen percent between 1991 and 2003. In fact, almost a third of the states do not require that elementary and middle-school students have physical education. At the high-school level, there are twelve states that allow students to meet their physical education credits with online courses.[18]

Organizations such as the American Alliance for Health, Physical Education, Recreation and Dance are among those lobbying to amend No Child Left Behind to include programs that foster a more active physical education program. This group has proposed the following changes in the law:

Hold schools accountable for providing regular physical education by including physical education in multiple measures for determining accountability.

Provide information to parents and the public by requiring all schools, districts and states to report on students' physical activity.

Ensure that children get the support they need throughout their educational experience (by encouraging more physical activity within NCLB program[s] such as Safe and Drug-Free Schools and Communities and 21st Century Community Learning Centers).

Support professional development for health and physical education teachers and principals to promote children's healthy lifestyles and physical activity.

Fund research and a pilot program to support effective ways to combat childhood obesity and improve healthy living and physical activity for all children.[19]

The influential Fox News Network has also chosen to highlight the importance of physical education. Like other sources, this program pointed to No Child Left Behind as being a major factor in reducing the time spent by students in these programs. Among other arguments, the story quoted a study concluding "that children who are physically active during the day in school are much more likely to be physically active after school as well."[20] Others believe that part of the problem is caused by the fact that No Child Left Behind defines the "core academic subjects [as] English, reading or language arts, mathematics, science, foreign languages, civics and government, economics, arts, history, and geography." Supporters of physical education and health programs are quick to point out that their subjects should be included on this list.[21]

As educators in all of these various subject areas criticize No Child Left Behind for the negative effect it is having on their programs, that effect is certain to be a major issue faced by Congress as it seeks to reauthorize the law. In this respect, it will only be one of a number of controversial issues upon which there will be a significant amount of lobbying by the interested parties.

Another such issue is the section of the law that requires schools to have only "highly qualified teachers" in the "core academic" areas.

NOTES

1. Jay Mathews, "English, Math Time Up in 'No Child' Era," *Washington Post*, 25 July 2007, www.washingtonpost.com/wp-dyn/content/article/2007/07/24/AR2007072402312.html.

2. Sam Dillon, "Schools Cut Back Subjects to Push Reading and Math," The *New York Times*, 26 March 2006, www.nytimes.com/2006/03/26/education/26child.html.

3. Peter W. D. Wright, Pamela Darr Wright, and Suzanne Whitney Heath, *No Child Left Behind* (Hartfield, Va.: Harbor House Law Press, 2004), 150.

4. Sean Cavanagh, "NCLB Could Alter Science Teaching," *Education Week*, 10 November 2004, aeoe.org/news/online/nclb-science-edweek111004.html.

5. Cavanagh, "NCLB Could Alter Science Teaching."

6. "Instructors Say Social Studies Suffering Because of No Child Left Behind Act," National Association for Bilingual Education, 22 January 2005, www.nabe.org/Clips/clip 012205.htm (accessed 16 April 2008), 1.

7. Dillon, "Schools Cut Back Subjects."

8. David Conrad, "American Music Education: A Struggle for Time and Curriculum," *Phi Kappa Phi Forum*, Fall 2006, findarticles.com/p/articles/mi_qa4026/is_200610/ai_n17195675.

9. "AFT Members Give Congress an Earful at Union's NCLB Town Hall Meetings," *American Teacher* 92, no. 1 (September 2007): 12.

10. Ron Whitehorne, "NCLB: Taking a Toll on Arts and Music Education," *Philadelphia Public School Notebook*, Summer 2006, www.thenotebook.org/editions/2006/summer/nclb21.htm.

11. Ron Whitehorne, "NCLB: Taking a Toll on Arts and Music Education."

12. Reynold Levy, "Putting the Arts Back in America's ABCs," in *Letters to the Next President: What We Can Do About the Real Crisis in Public Education*, ed. Carl Glickman (New York: Teachers College Press, 2004), 95–96.

13. Ellie Ashford, "NCLB's Unfunded Arts Programs Seek Refuge," *Education Digest* 70, no.2 (October 2004): 22–26.

14. American Music Conference, "Music Education May Be 'Left Behind' Under New Federal Requirements," 21 August 2007, www.amc-music.com/news/pressreleases/NCLB.htm (accessed 13 September 2007).

15. "Keeping Art Alive Under NCLB," Interview with Nina Ozlu, *Education World*, 11 October 2006, http://www.education-world.com/a_issues/chat/chat190.shtml.

16. Ken Rohrer and Judy Decker, "No Child Left Behind in a 'Nutshell,'" *Princeton Online*, www.princetonol.com/groups/iad/links/toolbox/nclb.html (accessed 13 September 2007).

17. National School Boards Association, "NCLB Is Putting Pressure on Foreign Language Programs," 18 January 2005.

18. Helyn Trickey, "No Child Left Out of the Dodgeball Game?" CNN .com, 24 August 2006, www.cnn.com/2006/HEALTH/08/20/PE.NCLB/index .html.

19. American Alliance for Health, Physical Education, Recreation and Dance, "No Child Left Behind," www.aahperd.org/aahperd/template.cfm?template=nclb.html (accessed 21 September 2007).

20. Jodi Noffsinger, "Phys Ed Cuts May Leave Children's Health Behind," *Fox News*, 20 November 2005, www.foxnews.com/printer_friendly_story/0,3566,176168,00.html.

21. Peter W. D. Wright, Pamela Darr Wright, and Suzanne Whitney Heath, *No Child Left Behind*, 65.

8

HIGHLY QUALIFIED TEACHERS

One of the primary purposes of the No Child Left Behind law is to ensure that our nation's teachers are all competent to teach the classes they are assigned. As we began the twenty-first century, there were many who questioned whether this was indeed the case in our country. Typical of the critics of the teaching profession was Thomas Sowell, who wrote in a book titled *Education: Opposing Viewpoints* that "most discussions of the problems of American education have an air of utter unreality because they avoid addressing the most fundamental and intractable problem of our public schools—the low quality of our teachers. There is no point expecting teachers to teach things that they themselves do not know or understand."[1]

He goes on to quote Rod Paige, who characterizes the system in place for preparing teachers as one that maintains "low standards and high barriers at the same time."[2] What Paige is suggesting is that one does not have to know much to be a teacher, but must go through all kinds of hoops in order to be certified. Both Sowell and Paige, like many others, are especially critical of required teacher education courses, which Sowell charges "have no demonstrated benefit on future teaching."[3]

Others pinpointed the problem of unqualified teachers to certain districts. While rich suburban schools had their pick of competent instructors, cities and some rural areas had serious problems recruiting and holding the best teachers. Duane Campbell wrote in 2002 that "we do not have a general education crisis in the nation: we have a crisis with black, Latino, and some Asian and poor white kids."[4] The problem of supplying competent teachers in 2002 seemed to be especially difficult for urban areas. Even when qualified teachers were hired, the turnover was extremely high. While some believed that the problem was lower salaries, others pointed to the characteristics of the students. The problem of turnover then and now in our urban areas is especially high among female teachers, who make up 75 percent of the profession. The Department of Education in 2002 reported the following:

- Schools serving academically disadvantaged students have more difficulty retaining teachers, particularly those early in their careers.
- Teaching lower achieving students is a strong factor in decisions to leave public schools, and the magnitude of the effect holds across the full range of teacher experience.
- There is strong evidence that a higher rate of minority enrollment increases the probability that white teachers exit a school.
- Salary issues need to offset the labor market disadvantages of certain schools.
- Schools with 10 percent more black students would [need to] agree [to] about 10 percent higher salaries to neutralize the [higher] probability of leaving.
- Similarly, a one–standard deviation decrease in school average achievement equates to [a need for] 10 to 15 percent higher salaries to hold exit rates constant.
- Women are clearly much less responsive to salary differences than men in determining whether to transition out of a school.[5]

It is also true that "new teachers on the average are lower performing than most experienced ones."[6] Because of high turnover, urban schools tend to have many more first-year teachers. In 2002, urban and many rural schools were unable to hire teachers who were certified by their state. Thus, these schools not only had more new teachers but also many teachers who did not have sufficient academic training in the classes they were assigned.

All of these factors led Congress to include in the No Child Left Behind law a mandate that teachers in core academic subjects be "highly qualified." Although states were given some latitude in determining how this goal was to be achieved, the law does include minimum requirements. According to the legislation:

> A highly qualified teacher must have an undergraduate degree and be certified or licensed by the state. Elementary school teachers must demonstrate knowledge of teaching math and reading. Middle school and high school teachers must have a major in the subjects they teach or demonstrate knowledge of the subject. Teachers who worked for school districts before 2002 must meet the highly qualified requirements by the 2005–2006 school year.[7]

Flexibility is allowed in the hiring of teachers for public charter schools. These instructors need to meet the requirements of their state's public charter school law. Many of these laws allow charter schools to hire uncertified teachers. A second area of flexibility is given to public-school teachers in the areas of science, multisubject, and special education. These exceptions are as follows:

- Science teachers are often needed to teach in more than one field of science. State requirements for science endorsement vary from a "broad field" science certificate to individual field certificates, such as for physics or chemistry. The demand for science teachers is high, so as of 2003, states may decide to allow science teachers to demonstrate that they are "highly qualified" with either type of certificate.
- Multisubject teachers do not have to return to school or take a test in every subject to demonstrate that they are "highly qualified." NCLB allows states to create an alternative method (high, objective, uniform state standard of evaluation, or HOUSSE) to certify teachers know the subject they teach. For multisubject teachers, HOUSSE requirements for each subject they teach are impractical. States may develop one process for current multisubject

teachers to demonstrate their experience, expertise, and professional training in a subject.

- Special education teachers who do not directly instruct students in core academic subjects or who provide only consultation to "highly qualified" teachers in adapting curriculums, using behavioral supports and interventions, or selecting appropriate accommodations do not need to demonstrate subject-matter competency in those subjects.[8]

Not only teachers are covered by the law; so are teacher aides or paraprofessionals. If they were employed after January 8, 2002, paraprofessionals in a Title I program "must have completed two years of college, obtained an associate's degree, or passed an assessment test." Paraprofessionals who were already working in schools when the law was passed were given four years to meet the criteria.[9]

To assist districts in meeting the prescribed requirements for paraprofessionals and teachers, the law mandates that schools earmark a portion of their federal aid for training purposes.[10] There are a number of options allowed for how these funds are to be used. For a number of reasons, meeting the requirements outlined by the law has so far been impossible for many districts. This became clear as the original deadline for meeting the "highly qualified teacher" mandate by the beginning of the 2005–2006 school year approached.

Beginning as early as March 2004, the Department of Education gave districts additional flexibility in meeting the requirement. Almost from the beginning, there were numerous complaints from smaller rural districts about this provision of the law. Approximately one-third of the school districts in the United States are considered to be rural. This includes districts with fewer than 600 students in average daily attendance or that have ten or fewer persons per square mile. Under the revised guidelines, a teacher who is highly qualified in one subject may teach in another academic area for three years, by which time he or she must meet the requirements of the law in the second subject. During the time they are teaching outside their area of qualification, these teachers must be provided professional development opportunities and intense supervision.[11]

Flexibility is offered to rural schools in areas such as science and social studies, where limited enrollment often requires that faculty members teach several subjects. In social studies, this would allow a teacher whose college major was history to teach classes in geography, economics, or political science. These guidelines also contain safeguards that attempt to ensure that the teacher has or is becoming qualified in the area.[12]

Two years after the introduction of No Child Left Behind, it became evident that rural schools were not the only ones that were having difficulty meeting the "highly qualified" criteria. This deadline was originally set for the beginning of the 2005–2006 school year. Because so many districts were unable to meet the timetable, the Department of Education has had to give schools additional time. These extensions have been "contingent on evidence that a state had been reordering its priorities and building the systems needed to take responsibility for the quality of its teaching force." In addition, districts were required to submit a plan as to how they would ensure that all of their teachers were highly qualified.[13]

When the original plans were submitted, those of the states of Hawaii, Missouri, Utah, and Wisconsin were found to be unacceptable by the Department of Education.[14] Although eventually all of the states did receive approval for their plans, it would appear that the overall goal will still not be met at the end of the 2007–2008 school year. By May 2006, nine states were being threatened with the loss of federal aid because they were not making sufficient progress on their plans. On the other hand, the Department of Education reported that twenty-nine states had made substantial progress. Thirty-three states had reached the 90 percent level in meeting the standards established by the law and by the state. The rest of the states were at percentages ranging from 70 to 89. CNN reported that the biggest problems faced by districts were in the areas of math, science, and special education.[15]

For teachers in areas with the lowest percentage of teachers meeting the mandated requirement, such as New York City, unusual efforts are being made to recruit fully certified teachers. New York has been offering a $5,000 housing incentive for teachers of math, science, and special education. The city will also pay tuition for career changers in needed fields to meet the certification requirements. New York City is not the only place that is offering financial incentives. For working in their lowest-performing schools, teachers in Los Angeles are being given a $5,000 bonus. Still, on August 15, 2007, the city had only hired 500 of the 2,500 teachers it needed to open school.[16]

States are using a variety of methods for filling their classrooms with qualified teachers. In Nevada, principals of "at risk schools" are being given first choice of the teachers that are being hired. Nevada is also offering additional credit toward early retirement to the teachers in these schools. Maryland's plan allows districts to lure back into the classroom retired teachers who can receive full pay and also collect their pensions. This provision is only used if they teach in high-poverty schools in a teaching field with a "critical shortage." Even though there is a variety of methods and plans, the Washington-based Education Trust contends that state strategies are "sprinkled with vague plans that lack the data to properly target the strategies or evaluate their effectiveness." This group, at least, believes that every state should be forced to draw up more realistic plans.[17]

Because the problem of hiring and retaining qualified teachers exists primarily in districts servicing poor and minority students, the Council of Chief School Officers published a summary of its recommendations for dealing with this problem. The group's recommendations are as follows:

Two goals:
- Increase the relative attractiveness of hard-to-staff schools so they can compete for their fair share of good teachers.
- Make these schools personally and professionally rewarding places to work.

Strategies that are MOST LIKELY to close the teacher-quality gap:

- Reward teachers for taking on more challenging assignments.
- Provide the specialized preparation and training teachers need to be successful in challenging classrooms.
- Improve working conditions that contribute to high teacher turnover.
- Revise state policies or improve internal processes that may inadvertently contribute to local staffing inequities.

Strategies that are *not likely* to close the teacher-quality gap:

- Involuntary transfers.
- Simply producing more teachers.
- Raising all teachers' pay (with conditions not changed).
- Purely compensatory measures to make up for bad working conditions, lack of resources, and poor leadership.[18]

Another problem, which is consistent with other issues related to No Child Left Behind, is the flexibility allowed to states in defining "highly qualified." Like the testing provisions of the law, there are variations between the states regarding the requirements for certification. For example, the examinations required in some states are different from those in others. Even when the national teacher's examination is used, the passing grade varies from one state to another. Certification classifications also are different among the states. In New York state, for example, there are different certificates for childhood (grades one through six) and early childhood (birth through grade two). Also, the certifications in New York for special education teachers include early childhood special education (birth through age two), childhood special education (grades one through six), and adolescence special education (grades nine through twelve), as well as an extension for middle-school special education certification. In addition, the state has a separate certification for those dealing with severe disabilities. Because of this myriad categories, the state has made it much more difficult to be certified.

To meet the federal government's HOUSSE standards, a wide variety of state policies have been developed. When the Department of Education has challenged certain plans, some states have fought back. In Connecticut, the qualifications of 13,000 of the state's 42,000 teachers were "thrown into question." The challenge in that state dealt with teachers in elementary school as well as those working with children with disabilities and in social studies electives.[19]

While some critics say that the plans being approved by states are excessively narrow, others suggest that the government is being lax in assuring that districts are employing qualified teachers. For example, Lynn Cornett, the vice president for policy issues at the Atlanta-based

Southern Regional Education Board, has criticized the law. For her, "experienced teachers have largely met the 'highly qualified' standard by taking a subject-matter exam with an unimpressive cutoff score for passing or by using the state's own evaluation, which usually awards points for experience and sometimes for such activities as travel and service on committees."[20]

Another group that has found fault with state attempts to ensure "highly qualified" teachers is the National Commission on No Child Left Behind. In its report, the commission charged that we were developing "minimally," not "highly" qualified teachers. As an alternative to the present methods, it suggested: "It is time to ensure that all teachers demonstrate their effectiveness in the classroom rather than just their qualifications for entering it. . . . Instead a new way of determining qualified and expert teachers must be developed—one consisting of multiple measures of student learning, teacher performance assessments and teaching practices evaluations."[21]

Because of the controversial nature of the effort to ensure competent teachers, various organizations have come up with other approaches for meeting the goal. Some examples of the suggestions are as follows:

- From the National Education Association: Pay more to teachers who agree to work in high-poverty schools for five years.
- From the Education Trust, a Washington research and advocacy organization: Require teachers to demonstrate student-learning gains to earn tenure after the first one to three years in the classroom; give significant incentives to teachers whose students learn the most to teach the most challenging students; devote the nearly $3 billion in federal Title II teacher-quality money to raising teacher quality in high-poverty schools.
- From the Aspen Institute's Commission on No Child Left Behind: Remove from high-poverty schools teachers who, despite professional-development offerings, rate in the bottom quartile of effectiveness as measured by student test scores for seven consecutive years.
- From several sources: Allocate Title II money to states that address problems with the recruitment, preparation, roles, and re-

tention of teachers; improve alternative licensure; and encourage new pay plans.[22]

Another approach being used to quickly fill our classrooms with teachers who have excellent academic backgrounds in their subject area is the development of alternative teacher certification programs. The purpose of these shortcut programs to certification is to allow individuals with majors in academic content areas to become certified more rapidly than they might have been in the past. These could be young people with liberal arts majors in academic subjects or career-changers who have decided to pursue the teaching profession. Such options often allow aspiring teachers to become certified in less than a year. Some of the programs that are sponsored by school districts actually offer financial incentives and possibly a guarantee of a job to qualified candidates.

This approach to preparing teachers emerged after the 1983 *Nation at Risk* report, which encouraged such plans. Specifically, the authors of the report refer to "recent college graduates with math and science degrees, graduate students, and industrial and retired scientists."[23] Teach for America is one of the best known initiatives in this category. By 2002, "forty-five states had initiated alternative teacher education programs." The federal government has allotted several billion dollars each year under Title II of the Elementary and Secondary Education Act for such programs.[24] New York state, by 2004, had already accredited twenty such programs, fifteen of which were being managed by colleges in New York City. There is now a National Association for Alternative Certification, which has its own journal and holds a national convention each year.

A study in 2007 was extremely critical of a number of these programs, charging that:

- Entry standards are abysmally low: Two-thirds of the programs surveyed accept half or more of their teacher applicants; one-quarter accept virtually everyone who applies.
- Rather than providing streamlined and effective coursework, about a third of the programs require at least 30 hours of education school courses—the same amount needed for a master's degree.

- Most disturbing, nearly 70 percent of alternative programs studied in the report are run by education schools themselves. Education schools have kept their market monopoly by moving into the alternative certification business.[25]

The report concludes with these words:

> In short, policymakers, reform advocates, and philanthropists who think they have "won" the battle in favor of alternative certification should think again. Twenty-five years later, concerns about the quality of education schools remain—as does the need for bona fide alternatives: swifter, better, surer, cheaper ways to address teaching aspirations on the one hand and workforce quality and quantity problems on the other. So put away the champagne. Much heavy lifting lies ahead.[26]

Linda Darling-Hammond also takes issue with the alternative program approach. In her writing she emphasizes that skillful teachers must know both their content and how to teach the wide variety of students they will encounter in their classrooms. Although often a critic of No Child Left Behind, Darling strongly supports the goal of improving teacher quality. For her, the appropriate model for the preparation of teachers is the method we now use to train doctors. Just as the federal government subsidizes medical education programs and teaching hospitals, she urges such opportunities for future teachers. In addition, her plan calls for scholarships for well-qualified candidates, along with "recruitment incentives" to "attract and retain expert, experienced teachers in high-needs schools."[27]

She goes on to call for money to pay for mentoring programs for all new teachers and a system of "high-quality teacher performance assessment that measures actual teaching skill." Her concern is that the typical written certification test only measures subject-matter knowledge, but does little to evaluate an individual's ability to teach. In assessing the final cost of her proposed "Marshall Plan" for producing high-quality teachers, she notes that such "an aggressive national policy on teacher quality and supply could be accomplished for less than the 1 percent of the more than $300 billion spent thus far in Iraq."[28]

Few would question the goal of providing highly qualified teachers in all of our classrooms. John Goodlad, in informal surveys, asked groups to identify from the four items listed below the one that they believed had the most promise for improving academic achievement.

- Standards and tests mandated by all states
- A qualified, competent teacher in every classroom
- Non-promotion and grade retention for all students who fail to reach grade level standards on the tests
- Schools of choice for all parents.

From an audience of about one thousand people at the 2001 National School Boards Association Conference, one person chose the first. All the rest chose the second, which usually is the unanimous choice, whatever the group.[29]

Undoubtedly, the issue of providing competent teachers is central to any effort to improve education in the United States. As a result, how Congress chooses to go forward in the effort to upgrade teachers will be crucial.

There are other such issues embodied in the No Child Left Behind legislation. Perhaps one of the most controversial is the question of school choice.

NOTES

1. Mary E. Williams, ed., *Education: Opposing Viewpoints* (Detroit: Thomson Gale, 2005), 44.

2. Williams, *Education: Opposing Viewpoints*, 44.

3. Williams, *Education: Opposing Viewpoints*, 45.

4. Williams, *Education: Opposing Viewpoints*, 49.

5. Jerry Aldridge and Renitta Goldman, *Current Issues and Trends in Education* (Boston: Pearson, 2007), 78–79.

6. Aldridge and Goldman, *Current Issues and Trends in Education*, 79.

7. Peter W. D. Wright, Pamela Darr Wright, and Suzanne Whitney Heath, *No Child Left Behind* (Hartfield, Va.: Harbor House Law Press, 2004), 25–26.

8. "What Makes a Highly Qualified Teacher Under NCLB," McGraw-Hill Education, teachingtoday.glencoe.com/howtoarticles/what-makes-a-highly-qualified-teacher-under-nclb (accessed 3 October 2007).

9. Wright, Wright, and Heath, *No Child Left Behind*, 76.

10. "What Makes a Highly Qualified Teacher Under NCLB," McGraw-Hill Education.

11. Michigan Department of Education, "No Child Left Behind Highly Qualified Teacher Flexibility Update," 30 March 2004, www.michigan.gov /documents/NCLB_HQ_Teacher_Flexibility_Update_88126_7.doc (accessed 11 October 2007).

12. Michigan Department of Education, "Highly Qualified Teacher Flexibility Update."

13. Bess Keller, "States Given Extra Year on Teachers," *Education Week*, 2 November 2005, www.edweek.org/ew/articles/2005/11/02/10reprieve .h25.html.

14. "Education Law Leaves Children Behind," CNN.com, 12 May 2006.

15. "Education Law Leaves Children Behind," CNN.com.

16. Sam Dillon, "With Turnover High, Schools Fight for Teachers," *New York Times*, 27 August 2007, www.nytimes.com/2007/08/27/education/ 27teacher.html.

17. Bess Keller, "In Every Core Class, a Qualified Teacher . . .," *Education Week*, 30 August 2006, 42–44.

18. Bess Keller, "In Every Core Class, a Qualified Teacher . . .," 42–44.

19. Bess Keller, "States Still Ironing Out 'Highly Qualified' Kinks," *Education Week*, 19 April 2006, 26.

20. Bess Keller, "NCLB Rules on 'Quality' Fall Short," *Education Week*, 16 May 2007, 1.

21. The Center for Teaching Quality, "'The Highly Qualified' Teacher or the Highly Expert Teacher," www.teachingquality.org/nclbhqt/index.htm (accessed 3 October 2007).

22. Bess Keller, "NCLB Rules On 'Quality' Fall Short," 1.

23. U.S. Department of Education, The National Commission on Excellence in Education, "Recommendations," *A Nation at Risk: The Imperative for Educational Reform* (Washington, D.C., April 1983), 5.

24. C. Emily Feistritzer, *Alternative Teacher Certification: New Support and New Urgency* (Washington, D.C.: National Council on Teacher Quality, 2002).

25. Kate Walsh and Sandi Jacobs, *Alternative Certification Isn't Alternative* (Washington, D.C.: Thomas B. Fordham Institute, 2007), www.edexcellence .net/doc/Alternative_Certification_Isnt_Alternative.pdf.

26. Walsh and Jacobs, *Alternative Certification Isn't Alternative*.

27. Linda Darling-Hammond, "A Marshall Plan for Teaching," *Education Week*, 9 January 2007, www.edweek.org/ew/articles/2007/01/10/18hammond .h26.html.

28. Darling-Hammond, "A Marshall Plan for Teaching."

29. Jack L. Nelson, Stuart B. Palonsky, and Mary Rose McCarthy, *Critical Issues in Education: Dialogues and Dialectics* (Boston: McGraw-Hill, 2004), 159.

9

NO CHILD LEFT BEHIND
AND CHOICE

The idea that parents and students should have some choice concerning their educational programs is not new. Economist Milton Friedman is often given credit for introducing the idea of a school voucher system as early as 1955.[1] During the years following this choice proposal, a number of models have emerged. In part to help integrate urban school districts, magnet schools were created, especially in large urban districts. These are schools like every other public school, but which provide to students a specific educational focus. For example, in cities all over the country, high schools with an emphasis on the arts or perhaps science are made available to the students. Other districts offer schools for outstanding honors students or perhaps vocational programs. Rather than attending a neighborhood school, families are able to choose or at least apply to have their children attend one of the district's magnet schools.

Another option for choice that has spread to many districts is known as open enrollment. If a district has six elementary schools, students are given a degree of choice in selecting the public elementary school within the district they wish to attend. Currently, the fastest growing type of choice is the establishment of charter schools. An idea that was originally strongly favored by American Federation of Teachers president Al Shanker, charter schools allow individuals, groups, or even private companies to gain legal permission from their state to develop semi-independent public schools.

The charters or contracts granted to these schools are given for a specific time period, such as five years. During that time, the school must demonstrate to the state that it is making sufficient academic progress with its students. Freed from most state regulations, these schools are allowed to establish unique programs to meet the objectives promised in the charter application. If they are successful in the eyes of the state, their charter can be renewed. Failure to meet the benchmarks agreed upon with the state could, and frequently does, result in the closure of the school. With the same budget per student as other public schools in the district at that level (elementary, middle, or high school), these nonreligious schools must open their doors to all students living in the district. If there are more applicants than the school is able to accept, a lottery system is often mandated.

Currently, almost every state allows the formation of charter schools. No Child Left Behind has encouraged this trend by providing facility financing for new and existing charter schools.[2] The law also offers assistance to magnet schools.[3]

More controversial than either the magnet or charter school option is Friedman's original conception of school vouchers. Although there are a number of varied approaches to the voucher concept, the primary aspect of the plans is to make available to families a voucher worth a prescribed amount of money for each school-age child. This voucher can be used to pay in full or in part the cost for a student attending a school chosen by the student's parents. Schools would use the money guaranteed by the government voucher to defray the cost of providing the student's education. Several of the voucher plans that have been proposed or are actually being implemented allow the participation of religious and other private schools. Opening this option not only raises First Amendment issues, but also produces a threat to the enrollment in the public schools. As a result, groups representing teachers, school administrators, and school boards have generally been strongly opposed to any voucher system that threatens public schools. They have been consistently supported in this position by most Democratic officeholders at both the state and federal level.

On the other hand, conservative Republicans have supported school vouchers. For them, forcing public schools to compete in a fair free-enterprise market would only enhance the quality in all schools. Arguing that public schools have always held an unfair advantage over private schools, many believe that vouchers would create fairer competition. The conflict between these two points of view was an issue during the debates over the initial passage of No Child Left Behind.

During his campaign for the presidency in 2000, George W. Bush labeled his position paper on education *No Child Left Behind*. Although this title was "cribbed from the liberal Children's Defense Fund," it emerged as a prominent Republican issue during the presidential campaign. Soon after the election was settled, the president elect invited to his ranch a group from Congress that included both Democrats and Republicans. Although he himself had been a supporter of school vouchers, he assured those at the educational summit meeting that vouchers "were not a make or break issue."[4]

Three days after taking office, the president sent to Congress a "30-page legislation blueprint" for education reform. It did contain "public school choice," and noted that "later, 'exit vouchers' toward private school tuition or for supplemental services were to be included."[5] When the debate on reauthorization of Title I of the Elementary and Secondary Education Act began, Senator Ted Kennedy assumed the leadership role in the Senate. The Democrats were primarily interested in boosting federal spending for educating poor children, and they were willing to compromise on some of the proposals of the Republican legislators. In order to get Democratic votes on the requirement for annual testing, it was necessary for the president and his congressional supporters to "give ground on vouchers."[6]

Although there was no national voucher plan included in the final version of No Child Left Behind, the legislation does contain several types of school choice. If a federally aided Title I school is unable "to make Adequate Yearly Progress for two consecutive years, its students are supposed to be offered school choice." This option allows them to attend another successful public school in their district. In making a choice, the parents could select a charter school within the district. This option would continue in subsequent years if the student's original school continued not to make adequate yearly progress. In the third year of failing to meet the mandated level of progress, a school must provide "supplementary educational services." These services are primarily some form of afterschool tutoring, which can be given by diverse providers, including private companies.[7]

These tutoring mandates must be paid for by the local district. If all of the schools in a district are designated as "in need of improvement," the "district is strongly encouraged to establish agreements with other districts that would allow students to attend schools in those districts not deemed 'in need of improvement.'" For the students who take advantage of the choice option, the district must provide transportation unless sufficient funding is not available.[8]

The guidelines for districts regarding transportation are as follows: They "must set aside 20 percent of the district's Title I funds for public school choice transportation and supplemental services. Of the 20 percent, 5 percent must be for supplemental services and 5 percent for choice transportation. The remaining 10 percent can be divided among the two."[9] If the 20 percent figure is insufficient, first priority must be given to "low income families."[10] To ensure that parents are aware of their options, it is required that schools notify them "no later than the first day of the school year following the year for which their school has been identified for improvement."[11]

Another provision of No Child Left Behind allows parents a choice of public schools within the district if their children attend a school that is labeled as a "persistently dangerous school." The method for identifying such schools is determined by each state. An individual student who has been a "victim of a violent crime on the grounds of his or her school is also eligible for school choice."[12]

With over five years of experience to consider, the choice options in the No Child Left Behind law remain controversial. Up to the present, it would seem that the law has not resulted in large-scale transfers of students. This was especially true during the first years after the passage of the legislation. For example, the Department of Education reported that "less than 1 percent of the 3.9 million eligible students used the public school choice option during the 2003–2004 school year."[13] Critics claim that the low level of participation was caused by "poor implementation" of the regulations by school districts. They pointed to the fact that "half of all school districts notified parents of the public school choice options *after* the school year had already begun." On average, five weeks had elapsed before parents knew that they could request a transfer.[14]

By 2005–2006, the numbers had apparently increased only slightly. A study conducted by the Council of the Great City Schools found that the number of transfer students surveyed had increased by 45 percent, but the percentage of those eligible for transfer who actually took advantage of the possibility was still below 2 percent.[15] Another problem that has emerged is that some popular schools that already have a full quota of students resist taking on additional transfer students. Advocates of choice are calling for "providing schools with incentives to accept transfers."[16]

Those supporting the transfer option feel that the state and federal government must do much more to enforce the parents' right to move their children. Of course in rural areas, especially in small school districts, there are often few options for transfers. One Department of Education official has suggested the controversial alternative of "allowing private schools to take part in the transfer program."[17] This idea was raised as a possibility prior to the passage of No Child Left Behind, and it will undoubtedly be revisited during the reauthorization debates.

Some districts have made serious efforts to allow for transfers. Portland, Oregon, by 2005, had allowed 1,000 students to transfer. This represented 17 percent of those who were eligible to change schools.[18] At the same time, it must be noted that around the opening of school in 2007, the *Washington Post* carried a story with the headline "Few Students Switching Under 'No Child' Law." The story reported that nationwide, "only about 1.2 percent of 5.4 million eligible children are taking advantage of the federal offer" and notes that to help districts implement the transfer option, the Department of Education had released a guidebook to "help schools inform parents about choice."[19] The story also reported that despite government encouragement, "research is not clear on whether switching schools is an effective way to boost student performance."[20] A limited study done by the Rand Corporation in 2007 found that there was "no measurable effect on achievement among students who transferred."[21]

The other choice option allows parents to choose supplemental educational services when their school fails to make adequate yearly progress for three consecutive years. Parents may select from state-approved tutorial services. As has been mentioned, this list can include both public and private providers. One survey in 2006 identified 1.4 million students eligible for tutorial services. Of this number, approximately 17 percent were actually receiving tutoring.[22]

It should be noted that any approved program must be "research based." Even with this requirement, an article appearing in *Education Week* in June 2007 claimed that "proof of the impact" of supplemental educational services "is sparse." By the 2007–2008 school year, it was estimated that half a million children would be receiving tutoring services. There have been a "smattering of studies," but none can conclusively prove the value of these programs. Some observers are calling for the Department of Education to fund a major study on the effectiveness of the supplementary educational services option. In looking for ways to strengthen this initiative, it has been suggested that "gains would be stronger if providers worked in tandem with their student's teachers. In several studies, teachers cited a lack of communication with outside tutors."[23]

Other problems include "student absenteeism and spotty implementation." The problem appears to be greater in schools with a high percentage of low-income students, where the percentage of eligible students receiving tutoring is disappointingly low.[24] While the program continues to have critics, most educators agree that one-on-one tutoring by a competent teacher is the best way to help students learn. Despite this consensus, there are several key questions that must be addressed regarding the future of supplemental educational services. Among these concerns are the following:

- Should the federal law reserve such services for students in the worst-performing schools, or should it expand the free tutoring to schools not currently qualifying for it?
- How should policymakers evaluate the businesses and nonprofit organizations that provide the tutoring, for as much as $2,000 a year per student?

- Should districts be required to spend 20 percent of their funding from the NCLB law's Title I compensatory education program for tutoring and school choice for students, even if there's not enough demand to spend all of that sum in one year?[25]

The Bush administration has also developed a proposal regarding the tutoring programs, which calls for the following:

Schools would be divided into separate categories depending on how far short of the AYP goals they fell for three years. "High priority" schools—those that missed their goals in all or almost all subgroups of students—would be required to offer tutoring to students eligible for Title I services. "Priority" schools—those that missed AYP for only one or two subgroups—would have the option of offering tutoring to Title I students.[26]

In addition, the president has proposed "offering supplemental services to schools that failed to make AYP for two consecutive years, shortening the eligibility time frame by one year.[27]

The whole topic of choice will be one of the most controversial areas in the reauthorization debates. It is an issue that divides the American public. Whether it be the practice of allowing parents to choose a private company to tutor their children or the more radical proposal of a voucher plan, the problem will be one that will emerge in debates between candidates at all levels. Democrats continue to be less supportive of choice options than Republicans. One might conclude that because of the Democratic Congressional victories in 2006, there will be less support for increasing choice options at the national level between 2007 and 2009. If nothing is done until after the election of 2008, the results of that vote could determine the fate of the choice options in No Child Left Behind.

While school choice is a controversial aspect of the law, another objective of No Child Left Behind is one that almost everyone can agree upon. This is the initiative established in the legislation to improve the security in our schools and to reduce or eliminate the impact of illegal drugs.

NOTES

1. Robert F. McNergney and Joanne M. Herbert, *Foundations of Education* (Boston: Allyn & Bacon, 1995), 249.

2. Peter W. D. Wright, Pamela Darr Wright, and Suzanne Whitney Heath, *No Child Left Behind* (Hartfield, Va.: Harbor House Law Press, 2004), 46.

3. Wright, Wright, and Heath, *No Child Left Behind*, 35.

4. Andrew Rudalevige, "The Politics of No Child Left Behind," *Education Next* 3, no. 4 (2003), www.hoover.org/publications/ednext/3346601.html.

5. Rudalevige, "The Politics of No Child Left Behind."

6. Rudalevige, "The Politics of No Child Left Behind."

7. Frederick M. Hess and Chester E. Finn Jr., eds., *No Remedy Left Behind: Lessons from a Half-Decade of NCLB* (Washington, D.C.: AEI Press, 2007), 7.

8. Candace Cortiella, "School Choice Opportunities under No Child Left Behind," Great Schools website, 1 January 2004, www.schwablearning.org/articles.aspx?r=778 (accessed 19 October 2007).

9. District of Columbia Public Schools, "NCLB FAQs," www.k12.dc.us/dcps/dcpsnclb/faq.html (accessed 25 October 2007).

10. Cortiella, "School Choice Opportunities under No Child Left Behind."

11. U.S. Department of Education, "Choice and Supplemental Education Services: Frequently Asked Questions," www.ed.gov/parents/schools/choice/choice.html (accessed 14 September 2004).

12. U.S. Department of Education, "Choice and Supplemental Education Services."

13. Dan Lips, "America's Opportunity Scholarship for Kids: School Choice for Students in Underperforming Public Schools," *Backgrounder*, The Heritage Foundation, no. 1939 (30 May 2006): 2.

14. U.S. Department of Education, "Choices for Parents: America's Opportunity Scholarship for Kids," February 2006, www.ed.gov/nclb/choice/schools/choice-parents.pdf (accessed 16 May 2006), xiv.

15. Hess and Finn Jr., *No Remedy Left Behind*, 47.

16. Caroline Hendrie, "NCLB Transfer Policy Seen as Flawed," *Education Week*, 20 April 2005, 14–15.

17. Hendrie, "NCLB Transfer Policy Seen as Flawed," 14–15.

18. Hendrie, "NCLB Transfer Policy Seen as Flawed," 14–15.

19. Maria Glod, "Few Students Switching Schools under 'No Child' Law," *Washington Post*, 27 September 2007, www.washingtonpost.com/wp-dyn/content/article/2007/09/26/AR2007092602368.html.

20. Glod, "Few Students Switching Schools under 'No Child' Law."

21. Glod, "Few Students Switching Schools under 'No Child' Law."

22. Hess and Finn Jr., *No Remedy Left Behind*, 51.

23. Debra Viadero, "Evidence Thin on Student Gains from NCLB Tutoring," *Education Week*, 13 June 2007, 7.

24. Viadero, "Evidence Thin on Student Gains from NCLB Tutoring," 7.

25. David J. Hoff, "Provision on Tutoring Raises Renewal Issues," *Education Week*, 8 October 2007, www.edweek.org/ew/articles/2007/10/10/07nclb.h27.html (accessed 25 October 2007).

26. Hoff, "Provision on Tutoring Raises Renewal Issues."

27. Hoff, "Provision on Tutoring Raises Renewal Issues."

(10)

SAFE AND DRUG-FREE SCHOOLS

Part A of Title IV of the No Child Left Behind legislation is titled "Safe and Drug-Free Schools and Communities Act." The purpose of this section of the law is the following:

> To support programs that prevent violence in and around schools; that prevent the illegal use of alcohol, tobacco and drugs; that involve parents and communities; and that are coordinated with related federal, state, school, and community efforts and resources to foster a safe and drug-free learning environment that supports student academic achievement.[1]

According to its supporters, using "research-validated effective drug and violence prevention programs," schools will be able to provide an academic environment in which students can best learn. The law makes available to states, communities, and school districts the possibility of obtaining competitive grants to support the following authorized activities:

- Addressing the consequences of violence and the illegal use of drugs, as appropriate
- Promoting a sense of individual responsibility

- Teaching students that most people do not illegally use drugs
- Teaching students to recognize social and peer pressure to use drugs illegally and the skills for resisting illegal drug use
- Teaching students about the dangers of emerging drugs
- Engaging students in the learning process
- Incorporating activities in secondary schools that reinforce prevention activities implemented in elementary schools.[2]

These grants must "be based on an assessment of objective data regarding the incidence of violence and illegal drug use in the elementary schools and secondary schools and communities to be served." It is interesting to note that private-school students can participate in these drug- and violence-prevention programs. In addition, it is mandated that the programs use "scientifically-based research" and "an analysis of the data reasonably available at the time." There must also be input from parents in the development of the application as well as the management of the program. One final requirement is that the activity must "undergo periodic evaluation to assess its progress in reducing violence and illegal drug use in schools."[3]

The provision of the law dealing with school security and drugs undoubtedly was included because there has been a continuing public concern that many of our schools are unsafe. Opinion polls have made clear that the public worries about lack of discipline and violence in and around our school buildings. Incidences such as the twelve deaths at Columbine High School in 1999 raised the level of concern about the safety of schools across the country. At the time of the passage of No Child Left Behind, data showed that there was some reason for concern.

In regard to student violence, in the same year as the passage of No Child Left Behind, "students between twelve and eighteen years of age were victims of approximately 1.8 million nonfatal crimes at school." This included 88,100 "serious crimes including rape, sexual assault, robbery, and aggravated assault." Even though these figures are alarming, it is important to note that the percentage of students who reported being victims of crime at school decreased dramatically between 1995 and 2003, from 10 percent to 5 percent.[4]

A new focus on bullying in public schools was also emerging. In 2002, "7 percent of students ages 12 to 18 had reported they had been bullied at school," while 15 percent of the students surveyed admitted bullying others. A new phenomenon called "cyberbullying" involves children being threatened via the Internet. Students using the "anonymity of the Web" are relaying "belittling messages, nasty rumors, and humiliating photos via e-mail and *blogs*."[5]

Another concern facing a significant number of schools is gang activity. The National Center for Educational Statistics reported that 41 percent of high-school principals and 31 percent of middle-school principals surveyed had encountered "discipline problems involving gang activity." In schools with this problem, it is three times more likely that a student will be known to bring a gun into the building. The presence of gangs tends to double the likelihood of violent victimization at school.[6] It also appears true that gangs are not found only in large urban areas, but have become more prevalent in small cities and even rural communities.[7]

An associated problem addressed in the law was the protection of teachers. In the five years prior to the passage of No Child Left Behind, "teachers were the victims of approximately 234,000 total nonfatal crimes at school, including 144,000 thefts and 90,000 violent crimes."[8] The U.S. government report titled *Indicators of School Crime and Safety* noted that "five percent of teachers in central city schools were attacked by students, compared with 3 percent of teachers in urban fringe and 2 percent of teachers in rural schools."[9] Perhaps the statistic causing the most concern for school districts is the fact that "more than 1 in 3 teachers say they have seriously considered quitting the profession, or know a colleague who has left, because student discipline and behavior had became so intolerable."[10]

While the statistics such as those mentioned above are sobering, it must be noted that in 2001 "nearly all public school teachers (98 percent) and most students (93 percent) report feeling safe in schools."[11] The situation also appears to be improving. In 1993, 16 percent of students in grades nine through twelve reported participating in a physical fight in school within the last twelve months. That number had decreased to 13 percent by 2003. Even more dramatic was the reduction of high-school students carrying a weapon in school within the past thirty days. That percentage went from 12 percent to 6 percent.[12] In regard to illegal drug use, a similar decrease is occurring. Still, the percentage of high-school students using alcohol and drugs remains high. At the time of the passage of No Child Left Behind, statistics showed the following:

- Forty-five percent of high school students admitted consuming one or more alcoholic drinks during the preceding thirty days.
- Twenty-eight percent of students acknowledged "episodic heavy drinking," which was defined as having five or more drinks in a row during the month preceding the survey.
- The percentage of high-school students who admitted using marijuana was 22.4 percent and 4.1 percent acknowledged the use of cocaine.[13]

One new trend is the use of Ecstasy and anabolic steroids. A final concern is the increased use of painkillers by teenagers.

Despite a seeming consensus that drug and crime problems in schools are declining, there is a fear that school officials are not reporting all of the incidents. Determining whether a fight between two sixth-graders should be considered an assault is a judgment decision. With so many adults, including police, supervising our school buildings, others have suggested that we have become overly strict in attempting to curb school violence. A 2007 report compiled by the American Civil Liberties Union titled *Criminalizing Schools: The Overpolicing of New York City Schools* claimed that "too much police involvement in schools" causes the learning environment to suffer. It goes on to suggest that minority children are most affected and that school safety "does not improve." The report claims that what is occurring is that students with behavior problems are being handcuffed and taken away as criminals.[14]

Similar criticism has been emerging concerning the "zero-tolerance" discipline policies that have been adopted in many school districts. Such an approach "typically sets out predetermined consequences or punishment for specific offences, regardless of the circumstances or disciplinary history of the student involved." For example, 90 percent of the public schools surveyed have reported zero-tolerance policies for students who bring firearms into school. Other schools have developed a similar disciplinary plan for such things as the possession of alcohol, drugs, and tobacco.[15]

One well-publicized example, which was highly criticized in the media, was the story of a six-year-old boy who was expelled for bringing to school with his lunch a plastic knife for spreading peanut butter. Because of the zero-tolerance policy, the school administration considered the knife a "weapon" and thus the boy was given the mandated penalty. Situations such as this have caused the American Bar Association to denounce "zero-tolerance policies that mandate expulsion or referral to juvenile court for minor offences that do not compromise school safety."[16]

At the same time that some critics are criticizing overzealous school districts, the No Child Left Behind law attempts to assist teachers and administrators in carrying out their disciplinary responsibilities by giving them some relief from potential legal actions. The provision known as "teacher liability protection" shelters school personnel from liability "if they are acting within the scope of their employment and do not violate Federal, State, and local laws." This section of No Child Left Behind shields school personnel from punitive damages unless there is "clear and convincing evidence that the harm was caused by an act or omission that constitutes willful or criminal misconduct, or a conscious flagrant indifference to the rights or the safety of the individual harmed."[17]

The No Child Left Behind legislation does not mandate specific discipline policies, but does attempt to give parents options if their children's school is considered unsafe. The section of the law that outlines this approach is quoted below:

> Each State receiving funds under this Act shall establish and implement a statewide policy requiring that a student attending a persistently dangerous public elementary school or secondary school, as determined by the State in consultation with a representative sample of local educational agencies, or who becomes a victim of a violent criminal offense, as determined by State law, while in or on the grounds of a public elementary school or secondary school that the student attends, be allowed to attend a safe public elementary school or secondary school within the local educational agency, including a public charter school.[18]

In addition to allowing students the choice of leaving schools that are deemed unsafe, the law attempts to be more proactive in helping districts to improve the social environments in their buildings. This has been done by making funds available for counseling, mental health programs, and character education.[19] Character education has become a very important initiative in public schools in recent years. These programs can become quite controversial. For example, an attempt to reduce unwanted pregnancies and the spread of AIDS might be pursued by either teaching abstinence, through instructions on birth control, or even the distribution of condoms in school.[20] No Child Left Behind refers to the attempt to integrate "secular character education into curricula and teaching methods of the schools." By using the word "secular," the law makes "a distinction from character education based on religious values." It gives the following examples of traits that could be considered secular character education:

- Caring
- Civic virtue and citizenship
- Justice and fairness
- Respect
- Responsibility
- Trustworthiness
- Giving[21]

The approaches to teaching these types of values are varied. The most common method, which began in our colonial days, has been labeled "traditional inculcation." Lessons were taught through teacher-centered classes often using a reading selection from books such as *The McGuffey Readers*, which were "replete with tales and poems of moral elevation." Today in schools, we use such methods as "values clarification." This program helps "students develop and eventually act on their values," by exploring various character traits and how they relate to their lives. Detractors of the method suggest that it fails to teach absolute values and as a result it is "valueless."[22]

Another approach uses concepts developed by Lawrence Kohlberg, based on the earlier writings of Jean Piaget. For him, there are specific stages of moral development. He believes that the earliest stages of character education should focus on simple rewards and punishments. Children learn right and wrong by striving for rewards or attempting to avoid punishment. As they mature, they grow to "higher stages of morality," which may even lead them to the highest level, acting on principle, which might result in civil disobedience.[23]

A more concrete approach is occurring in forty states that have been recipients of federal grants or have mandated that schools develop character education programs.[24] These programs "assume that there are core attributes of a moral individual that children should be directly taught in school." These values, which are the same ones mentioned in the law, are "encouraged through the school culture, conduct codes, curriculum, and community service."[25]

A significant aspect of the initiatives in character education, safe schools, and drug-prevention is the use of competitive grants. While grants can be helpful, it has been pointed out that smaller districts are often at a disadvantage in the competition for this money. In these systems, the administration is often limited to a superintendent, perhaps two or three principals, and a business manager. None of these individuals may have either the time or the expertise to prepare federal grant proposals. In larger districts, there are most often middle-level managers who have as their sole or primary mission to write grants. These individuals are specialists who have learned the art and science of grant writing.

On the other hand, it is possible that smaller districts may not have as great a need in the area of violence-prevention programs. James Garbarino, director of the Family Development Center, has written that "at the adolescent level, if I could do one single thing, it would be to ensure that teenagers are not in a high school bigger than 400 to 500 students."[26] Proponents of small schools say they:

> Create the opportunity for knowing students, for intervening as professionals before problems reach a crisis stage—before students resort to violence, suicide, or other forms of destructive behavior. In small schools, faculty can more readily share responsibility for recognizing and responding to troubled students and can designate the adults who will provide assistance. Simply stated, small schools obliterate anonymity—the handmaiden of many forms of youth violence—and create an environment where students are visible to those charged with their education and many aspects of their social and cultural development—their teachers.[27]

An article in the *Seattle Times* also emphasizes the importance of caring and watchful teachers. At the same time, it notes the need to foster student cooperation in creating a safe and secure environment in their schools. Kenneth Trump, chief executive of National School Safety and Security Services, has written that where school shootings have occurred, "there were fairly large groups of students who knew the person had a gun, had the intent, and made threats. . . . It's extremely rare that a shooter doesn't talk to anybody about it first."[28]

In dealing with possible violent acts, Judy Brunner and Dennis Lewis have made the following suggestions in an article published in *Principal Leadership*:

- Do not assume students will automatically come forward with important school safety information because "It's the right thing to do."
- Provide students with an anonymous reporting system.
- Periodically review the school's emergency response plan.
- Have a variety of individuals review the emergency response plan each year.
- Do not assume that local emergency service providers will be able to provide immediate assistance during a school crisis or emergency.
- Do not assume, as the principal, that you will be present or in charge during an emergency.[29]

These steps can make a difference if they are considered in all schools. The good news is that the various initiatives introduced in No Child Left Behind have caused an increased focus on reducing school violence and the use of illegal drugs, as well as on increasing character education. As a result, there is a good deal of evidence that the situation in many of our schools is better than it was in the recent past. Unfortunately, it is also true that in certain schools, especially in our urban areas, the situation is far from acceptable. The primary method for helping students in these unsafe schools is to allow them to transfer.

This procedure is undoubtedly in need of improvement. A report of the inspector general's office in the Department of Education concluded that the effort to identify dangerous schools and allow parental choice is "ineffective and in need of overhaul." Among other concerns is that "states have set the bar too high" for identifying unsafe schools. In 2006–2007, only forty-six schools of 94,000 nationwide were identified. Only seven states and Puerto Rico identified any such schools.[30]

In Ohio, for example, "under the state's policy, the inspector general's office concludes, a school with 1,000 students 'could experience four homicides and seize a weapon from students on 10 occasions each year without qualifying as persistently dangerous.'"[31] In June 2007, a report of the secretary of education's Safe and Drug-Free Schools Advisory Committee recommended that "schools cited as dangerous need targeted assistance, not just a punitive label." It also mentions the fact that the current label, "persistently dangerous," tends to stigmatize a school. The panel suggested a more neutral name be given to such schools.

They also recommend that a national system for identifying unsafe schools be developed. Another concern regarding school security is the inadequacy of the mandated emergency plans in some districts. Too many schools "have never trained with police, fire, and other public-safety agencies on implementing their plans."[32] These emergency plans have created a heightened concern about school safety, but the quality of the plans has been uneven.

Most of the initiatives instigated by No Child Left Behind have, on the whole, been helpful. As we look to the future, these efforts cannot be allowed to fade as we have not come close to meeting our goal of safe and drug-free schools and communities. It is certain that this objective cannot be achieved by dealing just with schools. Problems involving poverty, the decline of the family structure, and crime must all be addressed in a comprehensive effort if we are to improve our educational institutions.

One way No Child Left Behind hopes to deal with these very difficult issues is through faith-based initiatives and by allowing students to freely exercise their religious beliefs.

NOTES

1. California Department of Education, "Safe and Drug-Free Schools and Communities Act," 15 October 2007, www.cde.ca.gov/ls/he/at/safedrugfree.asp (accessed 2 November 2007).

2. California Department of Education, "Safe and Drug-Free Schools and Communities Act."

3. California Department of Education, "Safe and Drug-Free Schools and Communities Act."

4. J. F. Peter Devoe et al., *Indicators of School Crime and Safety: 2004* (Washington, D.C.: U.S. Departments of Education and Justice, 2004), nces.ed.gov/pubs2005/2005002.pdf.

5. L. Dean Webb, Arlene Metha, and K. Forbis Jordan, *Foundations of American Education* (Upper Saddle River, N.J.: Merrill, 2000), 263.

6. North Carolina Department of Juvenile Justice and Delinquency Prevention—Center for the Prevention of School Violence, "Selected School and Youth Violence Statistics," 2007, www.ncdjjdp.org/cpsv/pdf_files/statistics_2007.pdf.

7. William Christeson and Sanford Newman, *Caught in the Crossfire: Arresting Gang Violence by Investing in Kids* (Washington, D.C.: Fight Crime: Invest in Kids, 2004), www.fightcrime.org/reports/gangreport.pdf.

8. Devoe et al., *Indicators of School Crime and Safety: 2004.*

9. Rachel Dinkes et al., *Indicators of School Crime and Safety: 2006* (Washington, D.C.: U.S. Departments of Education and Justice, 2006), www.ojp.usdoj.gov/bjs/pub/pdf/iscs06.pdf.

10. "Teaching Interrupted: Do Discipline Policies in Today's Public Schools Foster the Common Good?" (New York: Public Agenda, 2004), www.publicagenda.org/research/research_reports_details.cfm?list=3 (accessed 8 November 2007).

11. *The Metropolitan Life Survey of the American Teacher* (New York: Harris Interactive, 2001), 39, 42.

12. David Miller Sadker, Myra Pollack Sadker, and Karen R. Zittleman, *Teachers, School, and Society* (Boston: McGraw-Hill, 2008), 159.

13. Webb, Metha, and Jordan, *Foundations of American Education*, 248–49.

14. Kimberly Ambrose, "School Safety Issues Bear Scrutiny," 5 November 2007, seattlepi.nwsource.com/opinion/338397_schoolsafety06.html.

15. Sadker, Sadker, and Zittleman, *Teachers, School, and Society*, 397.

16. Sadker, Sadker, and Zittleman, *Teachers, School, and Society*, 397.

17. Peter W. D. Wright, Pamela Darr Wright, and Suzanne Whitney Heath, *No Child Left Behind* (Hartfield, Va.: Harbor House Law Press, 2004), 70.

18. U.S. Department of Education, "Elementary & Secondary Education: Subpart 2—Other Provisions," www.ed.gov/policy/elsec/leg/esea02/pg112.html (accessed 25 October 2007).

19. Wright, Wright, and Heath, *No Child Left Behind*, 35.

20. Joel Spring, *American Education* (Boston: McGraw-Hill, 2008), 10.

21. Spring, *American Education*, 23.

22. Sadker, Sadker, and Zittleman, *Teachers, School, and Society*, 410.

23. Sadker, Sadker, and Zittleman, *Teachers, School, and Society*, 411.

24. Character Education Partnership Online, "Public Support for Character Education," www.character.org/site/lookup.asp?c=gwKUJhNYJrF&b=1049039 (accessed 18 May 2006).

25. David Carr, "Moral Formation, Cultural Attachment of Social Control: What's the Point of Values Education?" *Educational Theory* 50, no.1 (Winter 2000): 49–62.

26. Michael Klonsky, "How Smaller Schools Prevent School Violence," *Educational Leadership*, February 2002, 65–69, or www.ascd.org/ed_topics/el200202_klonsky.html.

27. Klonsky, "How Smaller Schools Prevent School Violence."

28. Nick Perry, "Watchful Staff, Students Key to Safety, Experts Say," *Seattle Times*, 4 January 2007, seattletimes.nwsource.com/html/localnews/2003508654_schoolsafety04m.html.

29. Judy Brunner and Dennis Lewis, "A Safe School's Top 10 Needs," *Principal Leadership*, September 2005.

30. Lesli A. Maxwell, "IG Report Questions Law's Unsafe-Schools Option," *Education Week*, 15 August 2007, 23.

31. Maxwell, "IG Report Questions Law's Unsafe-Schools Option," 25.

32. Alyson Klein, "NCLB Provision on Dangerous Schools Not Effective, Federal Panel Says," *Education Week*, 14 June 2007, www.edweek.org/ew/articles/2007/06/14/42safety.h26.html.

11

THE FAITH-BASED INITIATIVES

One might not expect to encounter a chapter devoted to issues of church and state in a book about the No Child Left Behind law. The fact is that there are sections of the law that address several issues related to religion in the schools. Church and state has long been a controversial question in the United States, with conflicts arising from differing interpretations of the First Amendment of the United States Constitution, which states in part that "Congress shall make no law respecting an establishment of religion, or prohibiting the free exercise thereof."[1]

The differences over the role of religion in public schools began at the outset of the effort to create tax-supported common schools for all children. When Horace Mann initiated the movement during the 1830s in the state of Massachusetts, he encountered opposition from Protestant Christians who had formed their own private schools. Their concern was that a public school could not teach Christian values. Needless to say, Horace Mann was successful in establishing non-denominational public schools in Massachusetts, and the movement spread throughout the nation. Still, in 1925, the very famous Scopes trial involved a teacher charged with teaching evolution to his students.

This was a violation of Tennessee law at the time because evolution appeared to contradict the creation story in the Bible.

It was not until much later in the twentieth century that a series of court cases attempted to clarify the constitutionality of such issues as prayer and Bible reading in public schools. A related issue that first emerged in the 1950s was the proposal for implementing a school voucher plan, giving to parents a sum of money that could be used to attend religion-based schools. This idea has increasingly gained the support of many Republicans, including George W. Bush. As we have seen, he supported such an option in his proposals for what became the No Child Left Behind legislation. There was not a voucher plan included in the final draft, but the law does contain several sections that attempt to give to religious organizations the ability to play a more active role in the field of education.

That goal is articulated in a government publication that claims that No Child Left Behind provides faith-based organizations ways to help in the education of children. Specifically, it mentions that funds are available for such groups "to provide tutoring and other academic enrichment services for eligible low-income students." It goes on to say that religious organizations can receive funds to help children in "reading, language arts and mathematics." Such programs can be held after school or can be early literacy offerings, mentoring programs, or even centered on technology. The Department of Education "provides free, user-friendly materials in English and Spanish that can strengthen the work of faith-based organizations."[2]

The plan to use faith-based groups to assist schools was very important to President Bush. Several days after taking office in January 2001, he issued an executive order that established a White House office "to expand opportunities for faith-based and other community organizations and to strengthen their capacity to better meet the needs in American communities." Approximately a year later, No Child Left Behind included provisions that "expanded the role of faith-based organizations by offering significant grants to them for providing educational services."[3]

As noted earlier, No Child Left Behind was the 2001–2002 revision of the 1965 law known as the Elementary and Secondary Education Act. The amended version requires the secretary of education "to issue guidance on constitutionally protected prayer in the public elementary and secondary schools." Such guidance had been offered earlier by President Clinton and was sent to superintendents in every school district. The document prepared by the Clinton administration was considered by many to be very friendly to those seeking a larger role for religion in our schools. The publication sent by President Bush's secretary of education, Rod Paige, went even further than the Clinton guidelines.

One difference between the two administrations was in the area of freedom of speech. For the Clinton administration, "the right of religious expression in school does not include the right to have a 'captive audience' listen." The guidance offered by Secretary Paige states that "the speech of students who choose to express themselves through religious means such as prayer is not attributable to the state, and therefore may not be restricted because of its religious content." Because the wording of Secretary Paige is not consistent with some court decisions, there have been legal observers who have suggested that the wording could place school officials in a difficult position in determining what students can and cannot say during public events such as graduation.[4]

Another difference between the guidelines created by the two administrations is that the Bush interpretation allows teachers and other school employees "to participate in religious activities on school grounds." The single most important change is a section in the No Child Left Behind law that forces schools to certify each year that they are protecting the right of free religious expression in their schools. Failure to certify or to follow these guidelines can lead to the loss of federal funding for the school district.[5]

In the instructions provided by Secretary Paige, there are specific directions that are meant to assist school administrators with certain potential conflicts that might emerge. These issues are noted below:

> Prayer During Noninstructional Time: Students may pray when not engaged in school activities or instruction, subject to the same rules designed to prevent material disruption of the educational program that are applied to other privately initiated expressive activities. Among other things, students may read their Bibles or other scriptures, say

grace before meals, and pray or study religious materials with fellow students during recess, the lunch hour, or other noninstructional time to the same extent that they may engage in nonreligious activities.

Organized Prayer Groups and Activities: Students may organize prayer groups, religious clubs, and "see you at the pole" gatherings before school to the same extent that students are permitted to organize other non-curricular student activities groups. Such groups must be given the same access to school facilities for assembling as is given to other non-curricular groups, without discrimination because of the religious content of their expression.

Teachers, Administrators, and Other School Employees: Teachers may . . . take part in religious activities where the overall context makes clear that they are not participating in their official capacities. Before school or during lunch, for example, teachers may meet with other teachers for prayer or Bible study to the same extent that they may engage in other conversation or nonreligious activities. Similarly, teachers may participate in their personal capacities in privately sponsored baccalaureate ceremonies.

Moments of Silence: If a school has a "minute of silence" or other quiet periods during the school day, students are free to pray silently, or not to pray, during these periods of time. Teachers and other school employees may neither encourage nor discourage students from praying during such time periods.

Accommodation of Prayer During Instructional Time: It has long been established that schools have the discretion to dismiss students to off-premises religious instruction, provided that schools do not encourage or discourage participation in such instruction or penalize students for attending or not attending. Similarly, schools may excuse students from class to remove a significant burden on their religious exercise, where doing so would not impose material burdens on other students. For example, it would be lawful for schools to excuse Muslim students briefly from class to enable them to fulfill their religious obligations to pray during Ramadan.

Religious Expression and Prayer in Class Assignments: Students may express their beliefs about religion in homework, artwork, and other written and oral assignments free from discrimination based on the religious content of their submissions.

Prayer at Graduation: School officials may not mandate or organize prayer at graduation or select speakers for such events in a manner that favors religious speech such as prayer. Where students or other private graduation speakers are selected on the basis of genuinely neutral, evenhanded criteria and retain primary control over the content of their expression, however, that expression is not attributable to the school and therefore may not be restricted because of its religious (or anti-religious) content. To avoid any mistaken perception that a school endorses student or other private speech that is not in fact attributable to the school, school officials may make appropriate, neutral disclaimers to clarify that such speech (whether religious or non-religious) is the speaker's and not the school's.

Baccalaureate Ceremonies: School officials may not mandate or organize religious ceremonies. However, if a school makes its facilities and related services available to other private groups, it must make its facilities and services available on the same terms to organizers of privately sponsored religious baccalaureate ceremonies. In addition, a school may disclaim official endorsement of events sponsored by private groups, provided it does so in a manner that neither favors nor disfavors groups that meet to engage in prayer or religious speech.[6]

The above guidelines were written to meet the requirement in the No Child Left Behind law that the Department of Education instruct school districts in meeting their requirements regarding prayer and religious activities in public schools. These instructions will change as a result of court cases and any new reauthorization of the law. The fact is that changes have occurred since the passage of the Elementary and Secondary Education Act, which initially required that the Education Department provide assistance to the schools in regard to their responsibilities related to religion.

One of the most important aspects of the church and state issue has been the section of the law that requires schools to provide "equitable services to private school students and teachers." Under Title I of No Child Left Behind, "participating school districts are required to provide eligible children who attend private elementary and secondary schools, their teachers, and their families with Title I services or benefits that are equitable to those provided to eligible public school children, teachers, and families."[7]

It is of course true that any reference to private schools in the law includes those sponsored by religious organizations. It has been determined through the years that services such as transportation, textbooks, and other learning aids, including technology and the cost for programs such as speech therapy and other educational services, should be provided for eligible private-school students in a school district. These students would also be eligible for health services as well as participation in vocational education programs at the secondary level. The same is true for remedial services financed by Title I of the current No Child Left Behind law. Most taxpayers are unaware that their local school district is paying for such programs for religious schools located in their community. The financial aid for these services is calculated in the same way as aid for eligible public-school students.[8] While this type of aid has been available to religious schools for many years, President Bush has been seeking to increase federal assistance to parochial schools. In 2005, the Bush administration agreed to help rebuild parochial schools damaged by Hurricane Katrina.[9]

In 2007, an article appeared in the *Washington Times* under the headline, "Bush NCLB Renewal Agenda Includes Parochial School Bailout." The story reported that the president would "try to prevent an increasing number of inner-city Catholic parochial schools from closing by adding funding for them in the upcoming renewal of the No Child Left Behind law." The article goes on to quote the president as saying that Catholic schools "have given millions of Americans the knowledge and character they need to succeed in life." In his justification, President Bush noted that "these schools are also serving thousands of non-Catholic children in some of the nation's poorest neighborhoods."[10]

The question of how much federal money should be available for religion-based schools is bound to be a topic discussed during the reauthorization process. In large part, these discussions will center on the issue of choice. There is already some support in Congress to expand school-choice options to include schools sponsored by religious groups. In December 2005, President Bush signed into law the largest voucher program in American history. The law set aside 1.6 billion dollars for the victims of Katrina. This legislation gave parents money to pay the tuition for attendance at parochial schools. The law allowed vouchers to be used for attendance at religion-based schools. Reg Weaver, president of the National Education Association, labeled the legislation "the worst assault on public education in American history." He went on to say that "for the first time ever . . . taxpayers will be forced to pay for a nationwide voucher program. . . . Religious schools will be allowed to receive taxpayer dollars, and proselytize and discriminate in hiring on the basis of religion."[11]

Washington, D.C., has also developed a plan that allows low-income families the choice to send their children to nonpublic religious schools. Close to 1,700 disadvantaged students have been given grants as high as $7,500 to allow them to attend the private or parochial school of their choice.[12] Choice programs such as those mentioned were declared constitutional as a result of a Supreme Court decision in 2002. The five-to-four decision written by Chief Justice William Rehnquist found that the voucher program initiated in the Cleveland public schools did not "constitute the establishment of religion." In the decision, the majority claimed that the "Ohio program is neutral in all respects toward religion. It is a part of a general and multifaceted undertaking by the State of Ohio to provide educational opportunities to the children of a failed school district."[13]

Not everyone agrees that this decision is good for education. As early as 1991, the chief Democratic sponsor for No Child Left Behind, Senator Edward Kennedy, said that "the important idea of educational choice should not become a death sentence for public schools struggling to serve disadvantaged students."[14] Needless to say, Senator Kennedy's concerns about the survival of public schools are shared by all of the groups with an interest in the public schools. Teacher unions, organizations of school administrators, and board of education groups form a solid front against additional school choice options, as well as increased financial support for religious schools.

While conservative Republicans may well push for more aid for parochial schools, as well as other additional school choice options, it is doubtful that a Democratic Congress and president would be so disposed. It is also likely that there will be additional court challenges to the current laws governing the relationship between church and state. In regard to No Child Left Behind, it would seem that the current federal courts are not likely to overturn any of the provisions of the law that relate to faith-based initiatives. At least one group that has studied these provisions and any relevant court decisions has concluded that "it is doubtful that the court will strike the provisions of the law down as unconstitutional. But, individual programs funded directly through grants will have to ensure that they do not violate the Establishment Clause."[15]

Assuming that the courts do not overturn any of the faith-based sections of the law embedded in No Child Left Behind, it might be assumed that the future of these provisions will be determined during the ongoing debates over reauthorization. One might venture to predict that a Democratic victory at the polls in 2008 that results in a larger majority in Congress and a Democratic president would limit additional faith-based initiatives as well as school choice options that might be considered harmful to the public schools.

Faith-based initiatives are not the only little-known aspects of the No Child Left Behind law. During the deliberations that occurred prior to its passage, congressmen and senators were able to include provisions that were important to them and to certain lobbying groups. Many of these sections of the law are designed to assist specific segments of the student population, while others represent concerns over particular political issues.

NOTES

1. Henry F. Graff and John A. Krout, *The Adventure of the American People* (Chicago: Rand-McNally, 1970), 803.

2. U.S. Department of Education, "No Child Left Behind and Faith-Based Leaders," 1 July 2004, www.ed.gov/nclb/freedom/faith/leaders.html (accessed 2 November 2007).

3. William Dolan, "No Child Left Behind's Faith-Based Initiative Provision and the Establishment Cause," *Journal of Law and Education*, January 2004, findarticles.com/p/articles/mi_qa3994/is_200401/ai_n9383391.

4. Marjorie Coeyman, "Religion-Free Zone?" *Christian Science Monitor*, 20 May 2003, www.csmonitor.com/2003/0520/p11s01-lepr.htm.

5. U.S. Department of Education, "More Local Freedom: Subpart 2—Other Provisions," www.ed.gov/policy/elsec/leg/esea02/pg112.html (accessed 25 October 2007).

6. U.S. Department of Education, "Guidance on Constitutionally Protected Prayer in Public Elementary and Secondary Schools," 7 February

2003, www.ed.gov/policy/gen/guid/religionandschools/prayer_guidance.html (accessed 28 November 2007).

7. Peter W. D. Wright, Pamela Darr Wright, and Suzanne Whitney Heath, *No Child Left Behind* (Hartfield, Va.: Harbor House Law Press, 2004), 85.

8. Wright, Wright, and Heath, *No Child Left Behind*, 202–3.

9. Alan Cooperman, "Parochial Schools to Get U.S. Funds for Rebuilding," *Washington Post*, 19 October 2005, www.washingtonpost.com/wp-dyn/content/article/2005/10/18/AR2005101801622.html.

10. Jon Ward and Natasha Altamirano, "Bush NCLB Renewal Agenda Includes Parochial School Bailout," *Washington Times*, 14 April 2007, www.interversity.org/lists/arn-l/archives/Apr2007/msg00119.html (accessed 30 November 2007).

11. Meghan Clyne, "Bush to Sign 'Monumental' School Voucher Law," *New York Sun*, 30 December 2005, www.nysun.com/article/25158.

12. U.S. Department of Education, "Secretary Spellings Delivers Remarks on School Choice," 5 April 2006, www.ed.gov/news/pressreleases/2006/04/04052006.html (accessed 5 December 2007).

13. Terry Frieden, "Supreme Court Affirms School Voucher Program," CNN.com, 27 June 2002, archives.cnn.com/2002/LAW/06/27/scotus.school.vouchers/index.html.

14. Susan Chira, "Bush School Plan Would Encourage Choice by Parents," 19 April 1991, query.nytimes.com/gst/fullpage.html?res=9D0CE3DB143BF93AA25757C0A967958260.

15. Dolan, "No Child Left Behind's Faith-Based Initiative Provision."

12

ADDITIONAL PROVISIONS

Contained in the hundreds of pages of the No Child Left Behind law are numerous sections aimed at addressing the problems of specific groups in our society. Many of these provisions are tied to the overall objective of the legislation, which is to ensure that all children in the United States receive the education they will need to succeed in the twenty-first century. One of the most immediate issues is the thousands of students who are dropping out of school prior to graduation.

No Child Left Behind requires that schools report annually on their graduation rate. This statistic is to include "only students who receive a regular diploma on time." In defining "on time graduates," the education department requires that "students have to complete one grade per year from the beginning of high school, which is usually ninth grade. . . . Students held back during high school to repeat a grade do not count as graduates."[1]

At the same time, these students are not to be considered as dropouts if they stay in school. There are problems in comparing graduation rates between different states. The guidelines issued by the federal government give to the states the latitude to develop differing methods of compiling graduation rates. A careful examination of the processes now being used by various states reveals that there is a lack of uniformity in the guidelines. It is also true that the law does not demand specific reporting on actual dropout rates. Even the graduation rate data that must be reported have little effect on the important adequate yearly progress (AYP) tabulation that determines whether a school is a success or a failure.[2]

A number of critics have found fault with the enforcement policies regarding graduation rates, and have suggested that it "stands in stark contrast to the rigid enforcement of test score accountability under NCLB." It has been suggested that the reliance upon test scores in calculating adequate yearly progress causes schools to "push out" poor students. In doing so, districts are able to raise their test profile. If indeed this is occurring, it is undoubtedly the minority students who are being harmed the most. Christopher Edley Jr., a professor at the Harvard Law School, has written that "the dropout/pushout syndrome is likely to grow worse unless the current exclusive emphasis on test-driven accountability structures in most states is balanced with more powerful incentives for schools to 'hold onto' students through graduation."[3]

The Charles Mott Foundation shares the fear that the way the law is functioning may cause "significant differences in graduation rates among minorities, the poor and other underserved communities" to go unaddressed. Duane M. Elling believes that "in the end, these young people are at risk of being left even further behind their peers." The extent of the problem is stated clearly by Christopher Swanson, director of the Editorial Projects in Education Research Center. He notes that "studies show that nearly one-third of all public high school students in the U.S.—and roughly half of all African-American, Hispanic and Native American students—fail to graduate in the traditional four years." He and others have called our dropout rate a national crisis.[4]

ABC News highlighted the dropout issue in a 2007 story with the title "1 in 10 Schools are 'Dropout Factories.'" The subtitle of this piece was: "Federal Government Puts New Focus on High Schools; Boosting Graduation Rates Top Goal." Nancy Zuckerbrod's story highlights the fact that our dropout rate has not improved during the last decade. She points out that most of the schools that are losing significant numbers of students are located "in large cities or high poverty rural areas in the South and Southwest," and that "most have high proportions of minority students." In addition, she suggests that the challenge of dealing with this problem will be greatest in these schools because of the need for additional social services for the students and their families.[5]

These so-called "dropout factories" are high schools or vocational schools where "no more than 60 percent of the students who start as freshmen make it to their senior year." Both the House and the Senate are considering amendments to No Child Left Behind that will provide additional funds to deal with the dropout problem. They also wish to put additional pressure on schools to improve in this area. The other possible change is to develop better definitions and an improved method for data collection regarding graduation rates.[6]

Although it is only one of many factors creating dropouts, the problem of developing effective education programs for English language learners (ELL) is another issue that was addressed in the No Child Left Behind law. The qualifications for defining these children are as follows:

An LEP [limited English proficient] (or ELL) student is an individual aged 3-21, who is enrolled (or about to enroll) in a U.S. elementary or secondary school and meets these two requirements:
    Belongs to one of the following categories:

Was not born in the United States or speaks a native language other than English;
Is a Native American, Alaska Native, or native resident of outlying areas and comes from an environment where language other than English has had a significant impact in the individual's level of English language proficiency; or
Is migratory, speaks a native language other than English, and comes from an environment where language other than English is dominant.

May be unable, because of difficulties in speaking, reading, writing, or understanding the English language, to:

Score at the proficient level on state assessments of academic achievement;
Learn successfully in classrooms where the language of instruction is English; or
Participate fully in society.[7]

Students who need additional education in the English language now comprise 10 percent of the population of our public schools. Between

1993 and 2003, the number of these students has grown 65 percent, while the overall student population has increased only 9 percent.[8]

Even though these children are only being introduced to the English language, they are required by No Child Left Behind to take most of the mandated tests. The major exception is that ELL students may be exempted from the language arts assessment. With the language arts examinations, they are excused for one year and allowed to take the test in their native language for three to five years. They are not given a similar exemption for math or science, although accommodations can be given to them as necessary. For example, these students can take these tests in their native language. Because we have students from so many different nations, this can only be done "to the extent practicable."[9] Of course, like other subgroups, the results of the tests taken by ELL students must be reported separately. Each state can determine how many students must be in a subgroup to require separate reporting.[10] Again, it will be urban districts, which have significant numbers of these students, that are most likely to be cited for failing to meet the guidelines of adequate yearly progress.

The fact that the 5.5 million ELL students in the United States speak more than 400 languages greatly complicates the problem for school districts. It is true, though, that 80 percent of these young people have Spanish as their native language. Title III of the No Child Left Behind law does allocate special funding for programs for ELL students. There are numerous requirements placed upon state governments and local school districts that wish to obtain these funds. The regulations include the following:

State Education Agencies Must:

Determine how they will define the ELL subgroup. The state may narrowly define the subgroup as only those students receiving direct, daily ELL services; or a state could define the group more broadly to include those students receiving direct services and students being monitored based on their achievement on academic assessments;

Explain in their Title III application how the state plans to increase ELL students' English proficiency in four domains: speaking, listening, reading and writing;

Describe how the state will align the above objectives with the challenging states academic standards [*sic*];

Consult parents when developing the annual measurable achievement objectives used to monitor the academic progress of ELL students;

Provide assurances that schools districts, education-related community groups and non profit organizations, parents, teachers, school administrators and researchers were involved in developing the annual measurable objectives for ELL students.

Title III Schools and School Districts Must:

Describe in their Title II[I] application to the state how the district has consulted with teachers, researchers, administrators, and parents, and others in developing their Title III plan.

Inform parents of a child identified for participation in a Title III program within thirty days after the beginning of the school year. For a child who enters school after the beginning of the school year, the school must inform parents within two weeks of the child's placement in such a program.

Communicate with parents in an understandable and uniform format, which means communicating the same information to all parents, and in a method that is effective.[11]

The problems inherent in dealing with ELL students are many and varied. Monty Neill has catalogued them in a paper prepared through the Iowa Department of Education. His list includes, in part, the following issues:

Most of these students attend schools that are already "lower-resourced." Because there is a "chronic lack of bilingual teachers," it is difficult, even if funds are available, for these schools to attract teachers from this limited pool.

Urban schools not only have more of these students, but they have a greater variety of languages to deal with. "Many ELLs are also racial-ethnic minority and low-income, some have disabilities, meaning they may count in two or more groups' AYP results. ELLs typically vie with students with disabilities for the lowest scores, further contributing toward multiple chances for a school to not make AYP."

The makeup of the ELL student group is always changing, as students frequently enter and exit the category. "This is compounded by the problem that students take five to seven years to obtain proficiency in academic achievement. Under this scenario, it is not reasonable to expect that in any given year all the students in the group will score proficient on the test. This guarantees that if there are enough such students for the group to count toward AYP, the school or district will fail."

Language proficiency tests have "low reliability" and therefore ELL classifications are often inconsistent.[12]

Finally, Neill argues that the sanctions called for under NCLB are "irrational." He suggests that it is unreasonable to expect students with limited English skills to compete fairly on English language tests even after three to five years of English instruction. It is his view that to punish a school for such failure is totally unfair.[13] There will undoubtedly be proposals made during the reauthorization process that will address some of these issues.

Yet another area that is likely to be dealt with in the months ahead is the question of early childhood education. There is a growing consensus that our nation must give additional attention to this area, and that doing so will have a very beneficial effect on our nation's education program. Part B of Title I of the No Child Left Behind act refers to the Even Start Family Literacy Partnership. The program is designed "to help break the cycle of poverty and illiteracy by improving the educational opportunities of low-income families." These programs are meant to "integrate early childhood education, adult literacy, and parenting education into a unified family literacy program."[14]

In a paper prepared in 2006 by Tom Grogan for the Wisconsin Department of Public Education, it is noted that "NCLB funding has had an impact, indirectly yet definitely, on such programs as Title I, Head Start, and Family Literacy." To increase the effect of the aid that is being given, Grogan calls for the following:

There should be a focus on the health of children. Students must be healthy to be ready to learn. Parents should be encouraged to have regular checkups for their children.

NCLB should help to create awareness and recognition of the importance of the foundation of skills and learning through early education. However, attention must be given to the problem that federal requirements can change how teachers establish requirements or expectations and that "high stakes" testing can create unwanted pressures to succeed before the child is fully able to perform at that level.

NCLB's focus on academic skills is not developmentally appropriate for young children; it has created age-inappropriate academic pressure on children. NCLB's focus on testing forces/encourages teaching methods that deny discovery and learning. Furthermore, the time spent on testing is time taken away from other activities (such as, hands-on or play-based learning).

An emphasis on the importance of reading is desirable; however, many preschoolers are not ready to read. Reading readiness skills must be strengthened in a play-based environment. Similarly, NCLB's accountability expectations may have an undesirable impact on efforts to meet the special needs of children with disabilities.

NCLB should ensure that early care and education providers receive appropriate professional development opportunities.

NCLB should ensure that parents receive support, encouragement, and resources to participate actively in their child's learning.

NCLB must reinforce, not hinder, best practices, particularly using age- and developmentally-appropriate approaches. The emphasis of testing should be reexamined: NCLB must find creative and instructionally sound ways to measure student achievement to use standardized testing, and to hold schools accountable.

NCLB should help to strengthen and improve compensation levels for early childhood education and care professionals.

NCLB should address the achievement gap that already exists by preschool age (low income/low literacy children at ages 3 and 4 are already behind). Unfortunately, some children will never be able to meet the benchmarks that are set even with a great deal of intervention. Furthermore, NCLB should address the issue of providing early childhood education and care for homeless preschool children.[15]

The fact that the cause of early childhood education is becoming more significant can be seen by the support of various political candidates for providing additional funds for this initiative during the reauthorization process. Hillary Clinton has proposed that a high-quality preschool program for every four-year-old be guaranteed by the federal government. She is estimating that the cost would be ten billion dollars.[16] The other Democratic candidate, Barack Obama, has recommended that the nation spend eighteen billion additional dollars on early childhood education, dropout prevention, and teacher incentives.[17]

A third targeted group is students who are categorized as homeless. Title X, Part C of the No Child Left Behind act deals with "homeless children and youth." According to the law, these children are described as follows:

The term "homeless children and youth"—
(A) means individuals who lack a fixed, regular, and adequate nighttime residence . . .; and
(B) includes—
(i) children and youths who are sharing the housing of other persons due to loss of housing, economic hardship, or a similar reason; are living in motels, hotels, trailer parks, or camping grounds due to the lack of alternative accommodations; are living in emergency or transitional shelters; are abandoned in hospitals; or are awaiting foster care placement;
(ii) children and youths who have a primary nighttime residence that is a public or private place not designed for or ordinarily used as a regular sleeping accommodation for human beings . . .
(iii) children and youths who are living in cars, parks, public spaces, abandoned buildings, substandard housing, bus or train stations, or similar settings; and
(iv) migratory children who qualify as homeless for the purposes of this subtitle because the children are living in circumstances described in clauses (i) through (iii).[18]

There are a number of services which can be financed to assist these students. Among them are the following:

- Before-school, after-school, and/or summer programs
- Outreach services to students living in shelters, motels, and other temporary residences to help identify homeless children and youth and advise them of available school programming
- Basic needs such as clothing, uniforms, school supplies, and health-related needs

- Counseling services
- The hiring of teachers, aides, and tutors to provide supplemental instruction to students whose achievement is below grade level
- Parental involvement programs that make a special effort to reach out to parents in homeless situations
- Data collection to assess the needs and progress of homeless and other highly mobile students.[19]

In December 2007, the federal Education Department published a twenty-page document designed to aid school districts in providing programs for their homeless children. The instructions for school administrators begin with the following items, which are listed as "the policy of the Congress":

Each State educational agency shall ensure that each child of a homeless individual and each homeless youth has equal access to the same free, appropriate public education, including a public preschool education, as provided to other children and youths.

In any State that has a compulsory residency requirement as a component of the State's compulsory school attendance laws or other laws, regulations, practices, or policies that may act as a barrier to the enrollment, attendance, or success in school of homeless children and youths, the State will review and undertake steps to revise such laws, regulations, practices, or policies to ensure that homeless children and youths are afforded the same free, appropriate public education as provided to other children and youths.

Homelessness alone is not sufficient reason to separate students from the mainstream school environment.

Homeless children and youths should have access to the education and other services that such children and youths need to ensure that such children and youths have an opportunity to meet the same challenging State student academic achievement standards to which all students are held.[20]

There is no question that Congress will be revisiting the issue of homeless children during the reauthorization discussions. At the time the original No Child Left Behind legislation was passed, there were, according to one source, 930,232 such children in the United States.[21] More recent estimates place the number at 1 million.[22] While problems

remain in finding appropriate ways to deal with these children, the law
has already been amended to allow homeless children to attend school
more easily. Formal barriers such as documentation of residency, im-
munization records, and birth certificates have been reduced or eliminated as requirements for enrollment in a public school.[23]

Along with providing for homeless children, Part C of Title I of the
No Child Left Behind law provides services for migrant children and
requirements on data collection concerning this subgroup. A migratory student is defined as:

> A child who is, or whose parent or spouse is, a migratory agricultural
> worker, including a migratory dairy worker, or a migratory fisher, and
> who, in the preceding thirty-six months, in order to obtain, or accom-
> pany such parent or spouse in order to obtain, temporary, or seasonal
> employment in agricultural or fishing work—
>
> A. Has moved from one school district to another;
> B. In a state that is comprised of a single school district, has moved
>   from one administrative area to another within such a district; or
> C. Resides in a school district of more than 15,000 square miles, mi-
>   grates a distance of 20 miles or more to a temporary residence to en-
>   gage in fishing activity.[24]

The law states as its purpose:

> To provide migratory children with high-quality, comprehensive educa-
>   tional programs;
> To reduce educational disruptions and other problems associated with
>   repeated moves;
> To ensure that schools do not penalize migratory children in curriculum,
>   graduation requirements and state achievement standards;
> To ensure that schools provide migratory children with educational ser-
>   vices that address their special needs;
> To design educational programs that help migratory children overcome
>   cultural and language barriers, social isolation, and health problems, and
> To prepare migratory children to make a successful transition to post-
>   secondary education or employment.[25]

Should a state fail to properly provide the required programs for
these children, the Department of Education can reduce or eliminate

federal funds allocated for such programs.[26] Examples of programs that might be created for migrant children include high-school equivalency preparation, early childhood education, parenting education, and adult literacy programs. In addition, there are grants for innovative programs that use technology in the education of migrant children.[27] As part of the implementation of such plans, the state and local school districts must document that they have formed and are actively utilizing a parental advisory council.[28] As with the other initiatives for special groups of children, it is likely that any reauthorization plan would maintain or enlarge the commitment to migrant children.

The same would be true for the provisions of the law devoted to Native American children. In the section of the law dealing with American Indians, the federal Department of Education provides that "families, tribal leaders and teachers" must be involved in planning. It also is noted that the "Bureau of Indian Affairs has its own accountability plan in place to ensure that its schools leave no child behind."[29] In the publication "How *No Child Left Behind* Benefits American Indians," the department claims that funding to help low-income Native American students has increased more than 60 percent under No Child Left Behind.[30]

A report by the Wisconsin Education Association disputes the Bush administration's claims that No Child Left Behind has benefited Native Americans. In a report titled *No Child Left Behind Leaves Native Americans Behind*, Molly Thompson argues that the law is forcing Native American children to become assimilated "into white, middle class culture." One parent is quoted as saying, at a meeting on Native American education, "The model of NCLB was created far away from Indian reservations and where Indian children live. . . . Our children see and order their world differently, and as a result, demonstrate their knowledge in deepening and unique ways." While some Native American schools have achieved progress with their test scores, Thompson charges that "it's at the expense and diminishment of Native language and culture" and that schools have also found it necessary to reduce or eliminate instruction in "educational aspects important to tribal history and tradition. Music, art, social studies and language are totally ignored." Finally, like other critics, the author complains about the failure to provide promised funding. Native Americans are unique in their opposition to the law in that many of them feel that it interferes with what they consider to be "tribal sovereignty."[31]

A publication of the National Education Association (NEA) also carries the headline "NCLB Leaves Native American Students Behind." The article quotes NEA president Reg Weaver agreeing with a report prepared by the National Indian Education Association and saying, "Labels don't help children learn. . . . American Indian children are internalizing the system's failures as their own personal failures."[32] A similar point of view is expressed in a portion of a letter that one Native American thought might be how Conassatego, an Iroquois leader in the 1700s, would have responded to NLCB:

> To the honorable members of Congress, We thank you again for the help you send to our schools but we must reject those requirements that are bad for our children and other children as well. The scientific method has limitations and should not be applied to all things. Indeed, its misapplication to the field of education may be hurting public schools across the nation.[33]

In defense of the No Child Left Behind legislation, Native American parents, along with the parents of every group of students, have been actively involved in carrying out the initiatives prescribed in the law. Parents are mentioned over 300 times in various sections of No Child Left Behind. One section of Title I of the law is devoted totally to parent involvement.[34] This provision mandates that every district and every individual school that is funded by Title I have a "written parent involvement policy." This policy must be developed with parental input and it is also required that it be distributed to all of the parents of children participating in Title I programs.[35]

Educators have long known the importance of the role parents play in a child's education. Few people would doubt the research that has concluded:

> The most accurate predictor of a student's achievement in school is not income or social status, but the extent to which that student's family is able to:

1. Create a home environment that encourages learning
2. Express high (but not unrealistic) expectations for their children's achievement and future careers
3. Become involved in their children's education at school and in the community.[36]

A study done at the University of Pennsylvania and the University of Michigan, for example, concluded that fathers have a major influence on whether their daughters have an interest in math. The same study concluded that parents tend to encourage their sons more than their daughters to develop interest in science and math. This is done as a result of toys that are purchased for their children, as well as by passing on stereotypes about the interest of girls in areas other than math and science.[37] Few would doubt as well that, in the area of language arts, parents who read to and with their children have a major effect.

Alluding to the decline of parental academic support for children, respected historian Diane Ravitch has written:

> The erosion of adult authority, fear of litigation, the decline of the neighborhood school, the lessening of community cohesion, and the loss of conviction within the education profession that schools should teach children the difference between right and wrong. As parents withdrew their responsibilities, the schools lacked the capacity to take their place.[38]

Recognizing the importance of parental involvement, the No Child Left Behind law requires that districts allot at least 1 percent of their Title I grant to programs involving parents. The law also mandates that each school district is to:

Provide assistance to parents of children served by the school or local educational agency, as appropriate, in understanding such topics as the State's academic content standards and State student academic achievement standards and State and local academic assessments.

Provide materials and training to help parents to work with their children to improve their children's achievement.

Educate teachers, pupil services personnel, principals, and other staff, with the assistance of parents, in the value and utility of contributions of parents, and in how to reach out to, communicate with, and work with parents as equal partners.[39]

Despite these requirements, there have been criticisms of the parental initiatives contained in No Child Left Behind. An article by Kent Allen in *U.S. News & World Report* begins with this charge: "Inadequate parental involvement is hindering the fulfillment of the federal No Child Left Behind program's goal to improve the nation's schools and produce better students." Allen lists the conclusions of a two-year research project conducted by the Appleseed Foundation:

> Too many parents don't learn NCLB-required data about their children and schools soon enough to make timely and informed decisions; that poverty as well as language and cultural differences impose barriers to parental involvement; and that such participation "is not uniformly valued by school leaders as a key accountability strategy."[40]

The National PTA organization has published a series of recommendations for Congress as it considers reauthorization of No Child Left Behind. With "nearly 6 million members in 25,000 local, council, district and state PTAs in fifty states, the organization is a strong lobby in the field of education at both the state and federal level." For the PTA, there are "Four Principles of Parental Involvement":

> More accountability to parents: Every state must designate an office or position, within their education department, responsible for overseeing the proper implementation of the parent involvement provisions required in the ESEA-NCLB. . . . Schools must provide opportunities for parents to be a part of decisions affecting school improvements. Whether that involves being an integral part of developing a school's parental involvement plan or evaluating proposed changes in curriculum, parents provide an invaluable perspective and need to be included in making these decisions.
> Better data through a more understandable delivery system: Federal law currently requires schools to provide information to parents regarding how well the school is performing. Schools must be required to provide the information from the accountability systems in language that is both clear and understandable to parents. As a critical part of making an informed, well-reasoned decision about the education of their child, the information must not only reach parents in a timely manner, but it must also be presented in a format and using language that is easy to comprehend.

Better resources to help teachers and parents: Teachers need better preparation on how to effectively communicate with parents and involve parents in their child's education, both at home and in the classroom. Through better preparation, teachers can be both promoters and beneficiaries of parental involvement, using their experiences to fully engage every parent.

Community Support: Schools must be an essential part of a community, working cooperatively to build partnerships within the community in order for the school to be more successful. Businesses and community groups need to be engaged and gain a renewed stake in every child's education. Federal law can support that engagement by providing incentives to encourage school-community partnerships. In addition, school-parent involvement plans must include community outreach and partnerships.[41]

As mentioned earlier, along with parents, another group that receives attention in the law are those individuals who assist teachers in the classroom. Paraprofessionals are limited by the law in the duties they perform. They are allowed to provide "one-on-one tutoring for eligible students if the tutoring is scheduled at a time when a student would not otherwise receive instruction from a teacher."[42] The reality of what paraprofessionals actually do in schools undoubtedly goes well beyond the parameters outlined in the law. There are still other concerns about the sections of the legislation that deal with paraprofessionals. Some worried that the regulations would create a "supply crisis." The problem was that many who have applied for these positions in the past did not have the required educational background and that those who were employed when the law was passed might decide not to meet the requirements by the 2006 deadline. This could have been especially harmful with the many bilingual aides necessary in urban school districts.

At the time the law was passed, only 40 percent of those holding paraprofessional jobs in instruction met the requirements under No Child Left Behind. Despite earlier worries, it appears that most districts were close to meeting the mandated deadline in January 2006. It was predicted that 95 percent of all schools surveyed by the Urban Institute would meet the deadline. Even in urban districts, it was expected that 90 percent of those holding these positions would be in compliance.[43]

The most common method used by states and districts for meeting the requirement was through the use of examinations. Such tests were offered to paraprofessionals "in 59 percent of rural districts, 74 percent of urban districts, and 89 percent of states surveyed." Unfortunately, it was found that some districts are "finding creative ways to bypass the spirit of the law in order to certify existing paraprofessionals." The Urban Institute suggests that "these districts may solve a potential short-term staffing problem but in doing so disadvantage themselves in the long run, as they miss an opportunity to train their teacher aides."[44] Assessing the effect of this section of the No Child Left Behind act may not be possible, but it is difficult to argue that it has not resulted in positive extra preparation for many paraprofessionals. This has been especially true for the large number of the aides who are helping students in the use of educational technology.

During the past quarter of a century, school districts have spent increasing amounts of their annual budgets to equip their buildings with computers and other forms of educational technology. No Child Left Behind has given significant financial support to this initiative. Part D of Title II of the law has as its purpose:

- to use technology to improve academic achievement
- to increase access to technology
- to ensure that every student is technologically literate by the end of eighth grade.

Grants can be used for such projects as:

- to create electronic networks and distance learning
- to promote parent and family involvement in education
- to facilitate communication between students, parents, teachers, and administrators.[45]

To gain funds for such projects, the school district must first "have an approved five year technology plan." They must also use 25 percent of any type of technology aid for professional training in technology. This training must give "special attention" to developing ways to integrate technology into classroom curriculums. The rest of the money can be used to purchase hardware, for distance learning, or for training courses for "master technology teachers."[46] It would seem that in meeting the technology goals of No Child Left Behind schools have made great but uneven progress during the past six years.

Unfortunately, it also appears to be true that technological progress has been slowest in some of our rural schools that have limited budgets. Part B of Title VI of the law does focus on the "unique needs of small rural districts, especially those with a large proportion of low-income students." Besides educational technology, Title VI funds can be used for teacher recruitment and retention, professional development, and parental involvement activities.[47]

It is estimated that 30 percent of the students in the United States attend rural schools and that 42 percent of all schools meet the description of rural schools used by the federal Department of Education.[48] Clifford E. Tyler has written specifically about the challenges of rural districts in adhering to many of the requirements of No Child Left Behind. Commenting on the major goal of meeting AYP mandates, especially the requirement to disaggregate the test scores, he notes that small numbers in the various groups can lead to statistically unreliable information. Data based on limited numbers can cause a school or district to be considered unsuccessful. He also notes that it might well "cause wild fluctuations in school-level test results from year to year."[49]

Because of low salaries and the remote locations of many rural districts, they also often have problems meeting the "highly qualified teacher" requirement of the law. The same is true with hiring and retaining paraprofessionals who have met the educational prerequisites of the legislation. Finally, the school choice options included in No Child Left Behind raise severe problems for rural districts. Since there are few other schools readily accessible for students who wish to exercise a choice option, transportation can become a critical issue for carrying out the school choice mandates.[50]

Along with specific aid allocations for groups and initiatives, there are several controversial miscellaneous provisions included in the law. These were clauses placed in the legislation at the behest of conservative legislators who were concerned about actions being taken or being considered by some school districts. One such section protects the Boy Scouts of America from discrimination by school districts. Because the by-laws of the organization discriminate against the involvement of homosexuals, some school districts had barred local troops from using their school buildings. Under the heading "Equal Access to Public School Facilities," NCLB states that any agency receiving federal aid may not "discriminate against any group officially affiliated with the Boy Scouts of America."[51] Even though this issue is not central to the academic goals of No Child Left Behind, it will undoubtedly be debated once again during the reauthorization discussions.

Perhaps even more divisive is the issue of the right of military recruiters to operate in public high schools. In an article that was originally published in the *School Board News*, Ellie Ashford writes that "the No Child Left Behind Act (NCLB) gives the armed services unprecedented access to potential recruits at a point long before young men and women in high school turn eighteen, the age at which they are required to register with the Selective Service." According to the law, military recruiters must be given the same rights to recruit in high schools as colleges. Schools must also give to recruiters the names and telephone numbers of students, unless their parents sign an "opt-out" form saying they do not wish to have this information given out. Failure by a school to meet these requirements can result in the loss of federal financial aid.[52]

With the help of the American Civil Liberties Union and other groups, schools all over the country have sought ways to challenge the requirement that military recruiters be allowed into schools. Because of the rising opposition to the war in Iraq, many parents are supporting this effort. An article in the *Christian Science Monitor* in 2005 highlighted the conflict. With enlistments down, it was suggested in the article that recruiters were becoming desperate. As a result, they were resorting to tactics that violated the guidelines of the military. As an example of the military's own concern about this, the Army suspended all recruiting on May 20, 2005, to "remind its 7,500 recruiters of proper conduct." At the time, there had been, in the previous six months, "480 allegations of recruiter improprieties."[53]

One year later, *Phi Delta Kappan* carried articles that also criticized military recruiting in schools.[54] Critics have also pointed to the fact that it is costing the government "close to $14,000" for every student who eventually enlists. It has been suggested that this money would be better spent on worthwhile programs for children.

Others have charged that "military recruiters often target people of color—particularly poor working class people of African or Latino descent—for recruitment."[55]

There is no question that the military recruiter clause of the law will be reconsidered. This is especially true as long as the war remains a divisive issue in our society. On this and other controversial issues, there have been hundreds of public and private groups contacting their representatives in Congress. Each of these groups has provided ideas for improving the law.

Despite the continuing support of the chief sponsors, President Bush, Senator Ted Kennedy, and Chairman George Miller of the House of Representatives, it would appear that as the nation prepares for the 2008 presidential election, the final passage of reauthorization legislation is still not in sight. At this point, it would seem to be helpful to attempt to understand why the process is taking so long.

NOTES

1. Christopher B. Swanson, "Ten Questions (and Answers) about Graduates, Dropouts, and NCLB Accountability," 21 October 2003, www.urban .org/url.cfm?ID=310873.

2. Swanson, "Ten Questions (and Answers)."

3. Chris Edley, "The Hidden Dropout Crisis," Center for American Progress, 27 February 2004, www.americanprogress.org/issues/2004/02/b35101.html.

4. Duane M. Elling, "Measurements Are Key to Addressing Nation's Dropout Crisis," Charles Stewart Mott Foundation, 29 October 2007, www .mott.org/recentnews/news/2007/cswanson.aspx.

5. Nancy Zuckerbrod, "1 in 10 Schools Are 'Dropout Factories,'" *ABC News*, abcnews.go.com/print?id=3790483 (accessed 6 December 2007).

6. Zuckerbrod, "1 in 10 Schools Are 'Dropout Factories.'"

7. Public Education Network and National Coalition for Parent Involvement in Education, "Programs of English Language Learners," *NCLB Action Briefs*, www.ncpie.org/nclbaction/english_language_learners.html (accessed 11 December 2007).

8. Northwest Educational Technology Consortium, "English Language Learners," *Focus on Effectiveness*, www.netc.org/focus/challenges/ell.php (accessed 6 December 2007).

9. American Federation of Teachers, "English Language Learners and NCLB Testing Requirements," www.aft.org/topics/nclb/downloads/QAELL0404.pdf.

10. American Federation of Teachers, "English Language Learners."

11. Public Education Network and National Coalition for Parent Involvement in Education, "Programs of English Language Learners."

12. Monty Neill, "Assessment of ELL Students under NCLB: Problems and Solutions" (Cambridge, Mass.: FairTest, July 2005).

13. Neill, "Assessment of ELL Students under NCLB."

14. New York State Education Department, "No Child Left Behind, Title I, Part B, Subpart 3, Even Start Family Literacy Partnership, 2005–2009," 10 March 2005, www.emsc.nysed.gov/funding/oldfundingopps/evenstart0509.htm (accessed 7 December 2007).

15. Tom Grogan, "'Voices from the Field': Observations and Comments on Early Childhood Education and Care, No Child Left Behind," Wisconsin Department of Public Instruction, 27 July 2006, http://dpi.state.wi.us/fscp/pdf/voices-frm-field.pdf.

16. Hillary Clinton for President, "Clinton Outlines Plan to Cut Minority Dropout Rates in Half," 27 November 2007, www.hillaryclinton.com/news/release/view/?id=4403 (accessed 17 December 2007).

17. Martha T. Moore, "Obama Unveils $18B Education Plan," *USA Today*, 12 November 2007, http://www.usatoday.com/news/politics/election2008/2007-11-20-obama-education_N.htm.

18. National Center for Homeless Education, *McKinney-Vento 2001—Law into Practice: Title I and Homelessness*, Spring 2006, www.eric.ed.gov/ERICDocs/data/ericdocs2sql/content_storage_01/0000019b/80/1b/c9/93.pdf.

19. National Center for Homeless Education, *McKinney-Vento 2001.*

20. U.S. Department of Education, "Elementary & Secondary Education: Part C—Homeless Education," www.ed.gov/policy/elsec/leg/esea02/pg116.html (accessed 4 December 2007).

21. Florida Department of Education, "The Education of Homeless Children and Youth (Title X, No Child Left Behind Act of 2001, The McKinney Vento Act)," Technical Assistance Paper 2005-007, August 2005, www.fldoe.org/bsa/title1/pdf/homeless_tap_08_23_051.pdf.

22. David Miller Sadker, Myra Pollack Sadker, and Karen R. Zittleman, *Teachers, School, and Society* (Boston: McGraw-Hill, 2008), 195.

23. Sadker, Sadker, and Zittleman, *Teachers, School, and Society*, 196.

24. Peter W. D. Wright, Pamela Darr Wright, and Suzanne Whitney Heath, *No Child Left Behind* (Hartfield, Va.: Harbor House Law Press, 2004), 271–72.

25. Wright, Wright, and Heath, *No Child Left Behind*, 262.

26. Wright, Wright, and Heath, *No Child Left Behind*, 265.

27. National Clearinghouse for English Language Acquisition and Language Instruction Educational Programs, "Migrant Education & the *No Child Left Behind Act of 2001*," www.ncela.gwu.edu/resabout/migrant/2_nclb.html (accessed 7 December 2007).

28. U.S. Department of Education, "Title I, Part C: Education of Migratory Children," 1 May 2006, www.tea.state.tx.us/nclb/newpolicy/title1c.pdf.

29. U.S. Department of Education, "Elementary & Secondary Education: How *No Child Left Behind* Benefits American Indians," www.ed.gov/nclb/accountability/achieve/nclb-amind.html (accessed 4 December 2007).

30. U.S. Department of Education, "How *No Child Left Behind* Benefits American Indians."

31. Molly Thompson, "Report: No Child Left Behind Leaves Native Americans Behind," Wisconsin Education Association Council, 13 October 2005, www.weac.org/News/2005-06/oct05/nclb.htm.

32. "NCLB Leaves Native American Students Behind," National Education Association, October 2005, www.nea.org/esea/nieareport.html (accessed 4 December 2007).

33. Robey J. Clark, "American Indian Tribes and NCLB—Should Tribal Governments Support the Law or Not?" buffalostonewoman.com/cce/ (accessed 6 December 2007).

34. Public Education Network and National Coalition for Parent Involvement in Education, "Parental Involvement," *NCLB Action Briefs*, 23 April 2004, www.ncpie.org/nclbaction/parent_involvement.html (accessed 7 December 2007).

35. Public Education Network and National Coalition for Parent Involvement in Education, "Parental Involvement."

36. San Diego County Office of Education, "Parent Involvement and Student Achievement," www.sdcoe.net/lret2/family/pia.html (accessed 27 January 2004).

37. Sean Cavanagh, "When It Comes to Math and Science, Mom and Dad Count," *Education Week*, 24 October 2007, 8.

38. Diane Ravitch, *Left Back* (New York: Simon & Schuster, 2000), 455.

39. New York State United Teachers, "Parent Involvement," 17 September 2002, locals.nysut.org/research/bulletins/2002nclb_parentinvolvement.html (accessed 7 December 2007).

40. Kent Allen, "Parent Involvement in NCLB School Standards Is Found Lacking," *U.S. News & World Report*, 27 September 2006, www.ctappleseed.org/pdfs/usnews.pdf.

41. PTA National Office of Programs and Public Policy, "PTA Recommendations for Parent Involvement in the Upcoming ESEA-NCLB Reauthorization," www.pta.org/documents/NCLB-rec07.pdf, 2.

42. Wright, Wright, and Heath, *No Child Left Behind*, 86.

43. Clemencia Cosentino de Cohen, "Crisis Brewing?: Paraprofessionals and the No Child Left Behind Act," The Urban Institute, November 2005, www.urban.org/publications/UploadedPDF/311269_crisis_brewing.pdf, 2.

44. Cosentino de Cohen, "Crisis Brewing?" 4.

45. Wright, Wright, and Heath, *No Child Left Behind*, 31–32.

46. American Federation of Teachers, "Technology Education," 25 August 2006, www.aft.org/topics/nclb/downloads/qatech.pdf.

47. Wright, Wright, and Heath, *No Child Left Behind*, 36.

48. Theresa A. Cullen et al., "NCLB Technology and a Rural School: A Case Study," *The Rural Educator*, Fall 2006, findarticles.com/p/articles/mi_qa4126/is_200610/ai_n16840814/.

49. Clifford E. Tyler, "NCLB: Tall Order for Small Districts," *Leadership* (Association of California School Administrators), September–October 2003, findarticles.com/p/articles/mi_m0HUL/is_1_33/ai_109738568/.

50. Tyler, "NCLB: Tall Order for Small Districts."

51. U.S. Department of Education, "Elementary & Secondary Education: Subpart 2—Other Provisions," www.ed.gov/policy/elsec/leg/esea02/pg112 .html (accessed 25 October 2007).

52. Ellie Ashford, "Conning Our Kids into Military Combat," *School Board News*, May 2005.

53. Dean Paton, "Rift over Recruiting at Public High Schools," *Christian Science Monitor*, 18 May 2005, www.csmonitor.com/2005/0518/p02s01-ussc.html.

54. William Ayers, "Military Recruiters Are Using and Abusing Our Kids," *Phi Delta Kappan*, April 2006, 594–99; C. T. Christine, "Not the Military I Know," *Phi Delta Kappan*, November 2006, 235–237.

55. Ken Schroeder, "NCLB's Trix Not for Kids," *Education Digest*, vol. 70, no. 2 (October 2004) 73–74.

⓭

THE BATTLE FOR
REAUTHORIZATION

From the outset, the No Child Left Behind law has had many critics. Several years before it was due to be considered for reauthorization, a commission was formed to study the effect of the legislation and to make recommendations on how it might be improved. Various interest groups formed cooperatives to add weight to their concerns and proposed numerous amendments for consideration. More than most laws, No Child Left Behind has directly affected the lives of millions of Americans, including students, teachers, and parents. Because of this, it has generated concerns in every state and congressional district. The mass media, as well as a vast array of educational journals, have also dealt with the law in great detail.

Criticism has come from many sources. There remain in Congress a number of individuals who voted against the law in 2001. For most of this group, their primary objection is that the federal government should not be attempting to manage the educational system in this country. These individuals might agree with the sentiment of Ronald Reagan, who suggested that the federal government did not solve problems, it was the problem. They would also be sympathetic to the argument that the founding fathers had meant to reserve the right to manage schools for the state and local governments. These individuals cannot be depended upon to vote for any reauthorization legislation.

This opposition reemerged in March 2007, when "more than fifty GOP members of the House and Senate—including the House's second-ranking Republican"—introduced legislation that would allow states to "opt out" of the law's testing requirements. The *Washington Post* suggested that such a change would "severely undercut President Bush's signature domestic achievement." This proposal has more sponsors than the number of members of Congress who originally voted against the law in 2001. In terms of the reauthorization process, the *Post* story quotes Representative Howard P. "Buck" McKeon, "the ranking Republican on the House Education and Labor Committee and a key ally of the president on the issue," as saying, "It was a struggle getting it passed last time. It'll be even more of a struggle this time." Although these members do not claim they wish to repeal the law, their position will make it much more difficult to find a compromise during the reauthorization debates.[1]

Along with the congressional opponents, opposition to the law quickly emerged from state governments as well as individual school districts. In the spring of 2004, fourteen states requested that the federal government revise a number of regulations that had been developed to enforce the law. The states claimed that "without any changes to the law, calculations suggest that within a few years, the vast majority of schools will be identified as in need of improvement."[2]

The state of Utah passed a resolution that gave its Education Department the power to "opt out" of the law even if it cost the state 100 million dollars of Title I money. By the opening of school in 2005, forty-seven states were in some "stage of rebellion" against one or more sections of the law. In twenty of the states, there had been at least some discussion about ignoring certain mandates of the legislation. The state of Connecticut had filed a major lawsuit claiming that the federal government had failed to provide adequate money to finance the mandates of the legislation. Even President Bush's own state was fined more than $440,000 for not fully implementing the law.[3] Within individual states, the law also created problems. For example, the school district in Reading, Pennsylvania, sued the state after a number of its school buildings were placed on the state's "warn-ing list" or the more serious "school improvement list."[4]

As noted earlier, the law became a campaign issue in 2004, when the Democratic presidential candidate, John Kerry, and his chief sup-porter, Senator Edward Kennedy, faulted President Bush for failing to keep his promises concerning the funding of the legislation.[5]

If there was opposition from the states and local school districts, there was also considerable unrest within the academic community. A consistent critic of the law has been Gerald W. Bracey, who in his an-nual report for *Phi Delta Kappan* magazine has defended the public schools and attacked the Bush administration's defense of the law. In his 2006 report, he cites a study conducted by Jaekyung Lee of SUNY Buffalo for the Harvard Civil Rights Project, which states:

> NCLB did not have a significant impact on improving reading and math achievement across the nation and states. Based on the NAEP results, the national average achievement remains flat in reading and grows at the same pace in math after NCLB as before. In grade 4 math, there was a temporary improvement right after NCLB, but it was followed by a return to the pre-reform growth rate. . . . NCLB has not helped the nation and states significantly narrow the achievement gap.[6]

Bracey is one of many educators who are concerned that the law overemphasizes the use of tests. He feels that "teaching to the test" will badly damage what is most effective in our schools. In defense of the flexibility that has often been present in our classrooms, he quotes Japanese visitors to our schools as saying, "Your schools have pro-duced a continuous flow of inventors, designers, entrepreneurs, and innovative leaders." These same visitors believed that the creativity of our teaching methods was a factor in making this possible.[7] Bracey also takes issue with Tom Friedman's best-selling book, *The World Is Flat*. He describes the book as containing "a golden treasury of un-documented, carefully chosen and just plain wrong statistics."[8] Fi-nally, in his 2006 report, he quotes a story written by Charles Murry for the *Wall Street Journal*. Murry wrote that No Child Left Behind was a "disaster for federalism" and contended that it "pushes class-rooms toward relentless drilling, not something that inspires able

people to become teachers or makes children eager to learn. It holds
good students hostage to the performance of the least talented, at a
time when the economic future of the country depends more than
ever on the performance of the most talented."[9]

Those educators who are associated with the so-called progressive
education movement, which resulted in large part from the ideas of
John Dewey, are among the most active critics of the No Child Left
Behind law. For school administrator and author Deborah Mier, the
central problem of American education is the need to ensure "equity
and justice for our most vulnerable citizens: the children of the poor.
. . . The real crisis facing the United States is social, not academic.
Children who come to school hungry and poor are not likely to be
helped by more rigorous standards."[10]

Well-known education author Jonathan Kozol began sounding the
same theme in a series of books talking about the inequality of education in the United States. Beginning with his best-seller *Savage In-
equalities*, written in 1991, he has helped to draw attention to the
need for helping students in poor schools. Kozol quickly determined
that to him, the No Child Left Behind law was the wrong way to help
these students.

The *Boston Globe* reported in September 2007 that Kozol had concluded that the law "has plunged urban education back to the dark
ages before desegregation. Under the law, schools whose test scores
don't improve each year could eventually be shut down, a specter over
a disproportionate number of city schools that educate mostly poor,
minority children." To dramatize his feelings, the seventy-one-year-
old "education warrior" went on a fast that by September 2007 had led
to the loss of thirty-two pounds. The *Globe* reported that Kozol
planned to continue this protest "until U.S. Senator Edward M.
Kennedy, who sponsored the original bill, agrees to drastically overhaul what Kozol called a punitive law that relegates urban schoolchildren to an inferior, stripped-down education and demoralizes
teachers, who he believes are forced to teach to the test."[11]

Kozol likens inner-city classrooms to "test prep factories."[12] For
him, success in our schools occurs when we have inspired teachers.
He has written that the best teachers he knows are "poets at heart who
love the unpredictable aspects of teaching and the uniqueness of

every child in their classes." These teachers, he believes, are "drawn to teaching children and not to business school. Teaching to standards that are not their own will make teachers technicians, and the classroom will lose its best teachers."[13]

Opponents of the law have been extremely critical of the Bush administration. This can be illustrated by a cartoon shown on the website NoChildLeft.com. The cartoon, which the site encourages its viewers to send to their congressional representatives, shows President Bush and perhaps Margaret Spellings watching a group of children who look like robots. Above them is a sign reading, "Mission Accomplished." The caption reads, "Their NAEP scores aren't any better, but we managed to kill science, social studies, art, music, library, recess, silent reading, thinking and problem-solving. Give us another four years and we will see better scores."[14]

While it would seem that the opposition will be formidable during the congressional reauthorization debate, the law continues to have important and powerful supporters. Although the reports on the improvement of test scores have fluctuated during the past five years, some of the more recent results have been more encouraging. The *Washington Post*, which frequently criticizes policies supported by the Bush administration, recently cited in an editorial a study done by the nonpartisan Center for Educational Policy. It suggested the results "should give pause to those who seek to derail reauthorization of the No Child Left Behind legislation." According to the editorial, the "exhaustive study . . . showed students scoring higher on state reading and math tests and narrowing the achievement gap between white and minority students. The pace of improvement increased after President Bush signed the legislation in 2002." The editorial went on to claim that "the law spurred schools across the country to focus on the qualifications and training of their teachers, to use data to drive instruction and to emphasize results." According to the *Post*, these policies brought "needed accountability to America's classrooms."[15]

The same results referred to in the *Post* editorial caused the Secretary of Education Margaret Spellings to suggest that the "study confirms that No Child Left Behind has struck a chord of success with our nation's schools and students. . . . We know the law is working, so now it is time to reauthorize."[16] The Senate sponsor of the law,

Edward Kennedy, was also positive, as he labeled the study "encouraging." Even the spokesman for the American Federation of Teachers congratulated members of the union "for the improvements in math and fourth grade reading."[17] ABC News also took note of the improved test scores in a story that graded the law on a number of its objectives. It suggested that "the state and national numbers on reading and math show some progress." Thus, in what the article calls the legislation's "central element," which is labeled "testing students to meet standards," No Child Left Behind was given an A-.[18]

The recent increase in test scores has bolstered the Bush administration's campaign in support of the law. Almost from the beginning, the administration has been arguing, "it is working and is here to stay." A White House press release from 2006 makes this argument thus:

The Theory Behind No Child Left Behind Is Straightforward: The Federal Government Will Ask For Demonstrated Results On The Investment It Makes In Education. Local schools will remain under local control, but instead of just sending checks from Washington and hoping for the best, we are measuring results and holding schools accountable for teaching every student to read, write, add, and subtract.

The No Child Left Behind Act Is Changing More Than The Law—It Is Changing A Culture. We are leaving behind the days when schools shuffled children from grade to grade, especially minorities and children who do not speak English at home. We are making it clear that every child can learn, and every school must teach. There can be no compromise on the basic principles of NCLB: Every student must read, write, add, and subtract at grade level—that is not too much to ask.

We Have Come Too Far To Turn Back Now—Reauthorizing No Child Left Behind Is Critical. If we were to lower standards and roll back accountability now, we would be abandoning children to the status quo that failed for decades, and the children hurt most would be the ones NCLB was designed to help—children in the inner cities, in rural America, and in special education.[19]

Additional support for No Child Left Behind can be found in the report of the Commission on No Child Left Behind, which was funded by the Bill and Melinda Gates Foundation. This report, titled *Beyond NCLB*, quotes the Center on Educational Policy, which states:

> Teaching and learning are changing as a result of NCLB. Administrators and teachers have made a concerted effort to align curriculum and instruction with state academic standards and assessments. Principals and teachers are also making better use of test data to adjust their teaching to address students' individual and group needs. Many districts have become more prescriptive about what and how teachers are supposed to teach. Some districts encourage teachers to follow pacing guides that outline the material to be covered by different points in the school year, while others have hired instructional coaches to observe teachers teaching, demonstrate model lessons and give teachers feedback on ways to improve.[20]

Despite these positive words, this report, like almost every other summary of the law, concludes that the legislation can and should be improved.[21]

The administration has its own ideas on how the law can be strengthened. A release in January 2007 describes the major initiatives supported by President Bush: the need to place additional emphasis on the high-school level and to "provide new options and choices for families whose children remain in underperforming schools."[22] In another publication, there is mention of creating "a Teacher Incentive Fund" that provides rewards to principals and teachers "whose students make exceptional progress." There is also support for providing additional opportunities for charter schools.[23]

The chief sponsor and supporter of the No Child Left Behind law, Representative George Miller, has also developed his own plans for improving the law. He agrees with the administration on the need for a "pay for performance" amendment for teachers.[24] This is a very controversial idea, as the teachers' unions have always been skeptical about the possibility of developing a fair system. This is especially true if the extra bonus is based largely on test results. In the monthly magazine *NEA Today*, NEA members are urged to write to Congress and say no to "pay-by-test scores."[25] While individual districts have negotiated plans that are currently being tested, this issue could be a major source of conflict during the reauthorization discussions.

Representative Miller also agrees with many other critics who suggest that schools should be rewarded for progress even if some of their students are below the desired levels. He suggests that the law should "differentiate between schools that failed on a broad scale and those in which one or two groups of students came up short, allowing solutions tailored to each school's specific deficiencies."[26]

Miller has introduced to his committee a list of comprehensive changes to the law. These proposals "came under sharp attack." Both civil rights groups and teachers' unions found fault with the draft that he presented. Among other concerns was a plan in the proposal for a pilot program that would "allow districts to devise their own measures of student progress, rather than using statewide tests." Civil rights groups were concerned that such flexibility would "gut the law's intent of demanding that schools teach all children, regardless of poverty, race or other factors to the same standard." Needless to say, leaders of both the American Federation of Teachers and the National Education Association protested any plan that would "count test scores in granting paid bonuses."[27]

Representative Miller's draft led to "fierce battles" on "virtually every proposed change" and appeared to "please no one." Describing the reaction, Amy Wilkins, an officer of the Education Trust, was quoted as saying, "His bill got creamed." Margaret Spellings, who has also been speaking in favor of a speedy reauthorization, admits that it faces "tremendous obstacles." She refers to the issue as a mine field.[28]

In an effort to bring about some sort of consensus, Senator Kennedy, in November 2007, invited the presidents of the National Education Association and the American Federation of Teachers to meet with him. After the session, both union presidents suggested that it "remained unclear whether Congress could produce a bill acceptable to union members." NEA president Reg Weaver said to the *Times* reporter, "I don't think you recognize the magnitude of the anger that's out there."[29]

Despite their criticism, both the National Education Association and the American Federation of Teachers support "overhaul, not repeal" of No Child Left Behind. For the NEA, there needs to be "a reduction in NCLB's single-minded, test-based, label-and-punish accountability system, coupled with the provision of funding proven programs that make a difference." For this group, a major concern is the formula for adequate yearly progress. In regard to the measurement of student learning and the evaluation of schools, the organization has stated that they "will not accept or support a bill that only offers tweaks and superficial changes."[30]

While the National Education Association and the American Federation of Teachers have begun a merger, which has actually been accomplished in some states, the leader of the AFT has also been vocal about the changes that his organization wishes to make in the law. In testimony before the Commission on No Child Left Behind, Edward J. McElroy, president of the American Federation of Teachers, has also pointed to the problems in the approach for determining adequate yearly progress. He told the group that the system "misidentifies as failing thousands of schools that are making real progress." In speaking about the overreliance on tests, McElroy quoted a teacher from Hartford, Connecticut, as saying:

> Over the course of this school year alone, my students have taken the Connecticut Mastery Test (eight days), the Stanford Test (three days), District Math, Science and Social Studies Assessments (twenty-four days so far), the 4-Sight Reading Test (ten days so far) and the SRI Lexile Test (ten days so far). This totals an approximate fifty-five days of testing. To this date, my students have spent an overwhelming 30 percent of their school year testing, and the academic year is still not over. That's one-third of their academic time not being spent on instruction but sitting in a desk taking a test.[31]

He also noted comments by union members who charge that the standardized tests they are forced to administer are too often not aligned with the curriculum they are asked to teach. Among the specific proposals McElroy made to the commission are the following:

- Extended school day and/or year programs for students who need extra academic help
- Reduced class size
- Early childhood programs.[32]

One of the problems raised by both of the national teacher organizations is the failure of the Bush administration to adequately fund No Child Left Behind. They are not alone in making this charge. Senator Kennedy has faulted the administration's budget proposal every year after the first year of the enactment of NCLB. Kennedy has put forward his own proposals for reauthorization. He, like many others, wishes to find ways to reward outstanding teachers, but does not focus on cash bonuses. He would provide teachers with "career advancement opportunities (additional pay with additional responsibilities) so that our best teachers can earn more money, move ahead, and serve as instructional leaders and mentors to new teachers." His goals also include creating a "better solution for low-performing schools."[33] Rather than criticizing schools, the law should "identify challenges and address them."

In doing so, the senator supports additional money for staff development opportunities for teachers, especially in lower performing schools. Like others, Kennedy would seek additional parental involvement in their children's education. He agrees with the administration on the need to place more emphasis on middle schools and high schools, especially in the area of dropout prevention. Finally, he wishes to ensure more rigorous state standards and take steps to improve student assessment.[34]

While there are numerous proposals for changing No Child Left Behind, there seems to be a consensus, at least in Washington, that with appropriate changes, the law should not be allowed to die. This opinion was expressed in an editorial in the *Washington Post* that began with these words:

> No one in his right mind would demolish his home because it had a leaky basement or it needed new carpeting. But that's the approach being advocated by those who find fault with the No Child Left Behind Act. The federal law is not perfect, but its architecture of educational accountability, transparency and equality is sound. With the law up for reauthorization this year, Congress should be debating how—not whether—to continue this landmark education initiative.[35]

Amanda Paulson, writing in the *Christian Science Monitor*, agreed as she pointed out that "even the act's harshest critics admit it has

changed the conversation about education in America, and has focused attention on poor-achieving groups of students who have been
overlooked."[36]

Although there are many members of the current Congress who favor reauthorization, public opinion concerning No Child Left Behind
could be turning against the law. Such a conclusion was expressed in
an article in *Education Week* titled "Poll Finds Rise in Unfavorable
Views of NCLB." The story is based on a survey completed by Phi
Delta Kappa International, which reports that "the public is evenly
split on whether the federal law helps or hurts schools."[37] Another
study, which was summarized in *Education Next*, found that on crucial aspects of the law, between 57 and 71 percent of those involved in
the poll favored renewal of the law as it is or with only minimal
changes. Perhaps the most surprising finding in this study is that 73
percent of those surveyed favored "one test and standard for all students" rather than "different tests and standards in different states."[38]
This result, if confirmed by other studies, might affect the debate on
this issue in Congress as to whether we should have state or national
standards.

While it might be true that a majority of the general public still is
somewhat positive about No Child Left Behind, a poll commissioned
by the New Jersey–based Education Testing Service found that 77
percent of teachers and 63 percent of school administrators surveyed
hold a "staunchly negative" opinion of the law. Even so, only a "small
percentage would dump it." On the question of national standards and
testing, this survey reported 59 percent of parents favoring such a
change. Only 43 percent of the teachers and 41 percent of the administrators supported this approach.[39]

The various polls that have been taken can be read in several ways.
The *Detroit News* chose a negative interpretation in an article that
featured the headline, "Most Americans Want 'No Child' Law Left
Behind." Careful reading of this article makes clear that when one
combines those who wish to abolish the law with those who wish to
amend it, it could be concluded "that nearly two-thirds of them want
Congress to rewrite or outright abolish No Child Left Behind." Of
that group, it is later noted in the article that only 14 percent of those
surveyed would abolish the law, while 49 percent wish to see it

amended. The single most negative conclusion of this survey, which was conducted by the Scripps Howard News Service, found that slightly less than half of those participating believed that the law "has had a negative impact."[40]

It is too early to gauge the current level of support for No Child Left Behind in Congress. Neither the full House nor Senate has yet to consider changes in the legislation. At the same time, No Child Left Behind has become a source of debate during the discussions on the 2008 federal budget. Although the 2008 fiscal year began on October 1, 2007, agreement on an education budget had not been reached by that date.

As with other programs in the budget, President Bush has been seeking to reduce domestic expenditures. In regard to No Child Left Behind, the administration points to the fact that the 2008 budget proposal offered by the president would represent a 41 percent increase in funding for education since he took office in 2001. The 2008 budget proposal put forward by the White House, however, provides for a 2.6 percent decrease for Education Department programs. The House has suggested a 7.8 percent increase, and the Senate, a 4 percent increase, over the 2007 budget.[41]

Beyond what he was proposing, the president made clear that he would veto any attempt to add funds to domestic programs. Concerning this position, Chairman Miller of the House Education and Labor Committee said that this veto threat "demonstrates that Mr. Bush isn't serious about working with Congress on a reauthorization of the law."[42] He went on to say that the president had "sharply reduced the prospects for good faith, bipartisan negotiation" over No Child Left Behind. In the statement, he noted that Bush "thinks he can have his education legacy on the cheap. He is profoundly mistaken."[43]

In part because of the budget stalemate, the *Los Angeles Times* noted in early November 2007 that the discussions on reauthorization appear to be "stalled" as a result of "wrangling of friends and foes." Despite this fact, No Child Left Behind remains important to its initial sponsors. Speaking about the president, House minority leader John A. Boehner has said that "it matters a lot to him."[44] This is understandable as No Child Left Behind could become the most important law passed during the president's eight years in office. It would seem that he would want to do everything he can during 2008 to find a way to reauthorize the legislation. At the same time, as the year begins, it would seem that there is a great deal to do before a reauthorization bill finds its way to the president's desk.

In any case, there's a provision in the law that says that the law will remain in effect as written until Congress acts in some way on reauthorization. Rather than accept changes he finds objectionable, the president may well decide to leave the present legislation in place when he leaves office. He has threatened to veto any revision "that would weaken the law's accountability requirements."[45]

There is no question that in 2008 the political focus will be on the presidential primaries and the race for the White House. As noted earlier, candidates have been careful with their comments concerning the law. Yet in November 2007, Hillary Clinton, while speaking at an elementary school in Waterloo, Iowa, said that the United States should "end" No Child Left Behind "because it is just not working." A *New York Times* article on the politics surrounding reauthorization also reported that Barack Obama was seeking "fundamental changes in the law." The third of the primary Democratic candidates, John Edwards, was criticizing what he believed was an overemphasis on testing. He was quoted as saying that "you don't make a hog fatter by weighing it." Because of the important influence of teachers and their unions within the party, any Democratic presidential candidate will be very cautious in dealing with the reauthorization issue.[46] On the other hand, the *Times* noted that "the teacher's unions have little influence with Republicans, and several Republican presidential candidates, including Mitt Romney, Rudolph W. Giuliani, and John McCain, have voiced support for the law."[47]

Although it is dangerous to predict anything in American politics, it would seem safe to suggest that sometime between the summer of 2008 and the end of 2010, a reauthorization of No Child Left Behind will be signed by whoever is president at that point in time. In the meantime, there will be a continuing national debate as to the content of the law.

It would seem helpful at this point to summarize the issues which must be resolved before an agreement is reached.

NOTES

1. Jonathan Weisman and Amit R. Paley, "Dozens in GOP Turn Against Bush's Prized 'No Child' Act," *Washington Post*, 15 March 2007, www .washingtonpost.com/wpdyn/content/article/2007/03/14/AR2007031402741. html.

2. John Merrow, *Choosing Excellence* (Lanham, Md.: Scarecrow Press, 2001), 121–23.

3. Kavan Peterson, "No Letup in Unrest over Bush School Law," *Stateline.org*, 7 July 2005, www.stateline.org/live/ViewPage.action?siteNodeId= 136&contentId=41610 (accessed 4 August 2005).

4. Myra Pollack Sadker and David Miller Sadker, *Teachers, Schools, and Society* (Boston: McGraw-Hill, 2003), 47–48.

5. "Bush Makes Money, Touts Education," CNN.com, 6 January 2004, www.cnn.com/2004/ALLPOLITICS/01/06/elec04.prez.bush.fundraising.ap/.

6. Gerald W. Bracey, "The 16th Bracey Report on the Condition of Public Education," *Phi Delta Kappan*, October 2006, 151–66 or www.americatomorrow.com/bracey/EDDRA/k0610bra.pdf.

7. Joseph Renzulli, "A Quiet Crisis Is Clouding the Future of R & D," *Education Week*, 25 May 2005, 32–33.

8. Bracey, "The 16th Bracey Report," 154.

9. Bracey, "The 16th Bracey Report," 159.

10. Jack L. Nelson, Stuart B. Palonsky, and Mary Rose McCarthy, *Critical Issues in Education: Dialogues and Dialectics* (Boston: McGraw-Hill, 2004), 165.

11. Tracy Jan, "Reading, Writing, and Rebellion," *Boston Globe*, 21 September 2007, www.boston.com/news/local/articles/2007/09/21/reading_writing _and_rebellion.

12. Jan, "Reading, Writing, and Rebellion."

13. Nelson, Palonsky, and McCarthy, *Critical Issues in Education*, 163.

14. Jerry King, "Mission Accomplished," FNO Press, 2006, nochildleft .com/cartoon46.html.

15. "Measurable Progress in School," *Washington Post*, National Weekly Edition, 8 July 2007, 29.

16. Amit R. Paley, "No Child Left Behind Law Aiding Test Scores?" *Seattle Times*, 6 June 2007, seattletimes.nwsource.com/html/nationworld/ 2003736070_nochild06.html.

17. Sam Dillon, "Math Scores Rise, but Reading Is Mixed," *New York Times*, 26 September 2007.

18. "Report Card: No Child Left Behind," *ABC News*, 29 May 2007, abcnews.go.com/GMA/Politics/story?id=3221230.

19. The White House, "Fact Sheet: The No Child Left Behind Act: Challenging Students Through High Expectations," 5 October 2006, www .whitehouse.gov/news/releases/2006/10/20061005-2.html (accessed 5 December 2007).

20. Secretary Tommy G. Thompson and Governor Roy E. Barnes, *Beyond NCLB: Fulfilling the Promise to Our Nation's Children* (Washington, D.C.: Aspen Institute, 2007), 16.

21. Thompson, and Barnes, *Beyond NCLB*, 16–20.

22. U.S. Department of Education, "Secretary Spellings Launches Priorities for NCLB Reauthorization," 24 January 2007, www.ed.gov/news/ pressreleases/2007/01/01242007.html (accessed 5 December 2007).

23. Margaret Spellings, *Building on Results: A Blueprint for Strengthening the No Child Left Behind Act* (Jessup, Md.: Education Publications Center, 2007), 5.

24. Diana Jean Schemo, "Crucial Lawmaker Outlines Changes to Education Law," *New York Times*, 31 July 2007, www.nytimes.com/2007/07/31/ washington/31child.html.

25. National Education Association, "Let's Get Loud: Make Your Voice Heard NOW!" *NEA Today*, January 2008, 13.

26. Schemo, "Crucial Lawmaker Outlines Changes to Education Law."

27. Diana Jean Schemo, "Teachers and Rights Groups Oppose Education Measure," *New York Times*, 11 September 2007, www.nytimes.com/ 2007/09/11/education/11child.html.

28. Sam Dillon, "Democrats Make Bush School Act an Election Issue," *New York Times*, 23 December 2007, www.nytimes.com/2007/12/23/us/politics/ 23child.html.

29. Dillon, "Democrats Make Bush School Act an Election Issue."

30. Joel Packer, "The NEA Is Fighting for NCLB Overhaul," *Phi Delta Kappan*, December 2007, 275–77.

31. Edward J. McElroy, "Testimony of Edward J. McElroy, President, American Federation of Teachers, Before the Commission on No Child Left Behind," 25 September 2006, Washington, D.C., 2.

32. McElroy, "Testimony of Edward J. McElroy, President, American Federation of Teachers, Before the Commission on No Child Left Behind," 2–3.

33. Senator Edward M. Kennedy, "Kennedy Outlines Agenda for NCLB Reauthorization at National School Boards Association Conference," 29 January 2007, National School Boards Legislative Conference.

34. Kennedy, "Kennedy Outlines Agenda for NCLB Reauthorization."

35. "'No Child' in the Crosshairs," *Washington Post*, editorial, 2 July 2007, www.washingtonpost.com/wp-dyn/content/article/2007/07/01/AR2007070100905.html.

36. Amanda Paulson, "Next Round Begins for No Child Left Behind," *Christian Science Monitor*, 8 January 2007, www.csmonitor.com/2007/0108/p01s01-uspo.html.

37. Andrew Trotter, "Poll Finds Rise in Unfavorable Views of NCLB," *Education Week*, 29 August 2007, 10.

38. William G. Howell, Martin R. West, and Paul E. Peterson, "What Americans Think about Their Schools: The 2007 Education Next—PEPG Survey," *Education Next* 7, no. 4 (2007), www.hoover.org/publications/ednext/8769517.html.

39. Howard Blume, "Parents, Educators Split on What to Do with No Child Left Behind," *Los Angeles Times*, 25 June 2007, www.districtadministration.com/newssummary.aspx?news=yes&postid=19397.

40. Scripps Howard News Service, "Most Americans Want 'No Child' Law Left Behind," *Detroit News*, 31 May 2007.

41. Alyson Klein, "Bush, Democrats Face Education Spending Showdown," *Education Week*, 19 October 2007, www.edweek.org/ew/articles/2007/10/24/09budget.h27.html.

42. Alyson Klein, "Jousting Continues over Budget Increase for Education," *Education Week*, 14 November 2007, 24.

43. Klein, "Jousting Continues over Budget Increase for Education," 24.

44. "No Child Left Behind Looks to Be Stalled," *Washington Post*, 5 November 2007, 4lakidsnews.blogspot.com/2007/11/no-child-left-behind-looks-to-be.html.

45. Alyson Klein, "Spellings Offers Guidance to Help Clarify Privacy Law," *Education Week*, 7 November 2007, 22.

46. Dillon, "Democrats Make Bush School Act an Election Issue."

47. Dillon, "Democrats Make Bush School Act an Election Issue."

III

THE FUTURE

⑭

THE ISSUES

The aspect of No Child Left Behind that everyone agrees upon is described in the name given to the law. Who can object to the goal of having no child left behind? Everyone can support the notion that our schools should be seeking to ensure that all students learn up to their maximum potential. Beyond that, there are those who find fault with most of the initiatives that the legislation uses to reach this objective. These many criticisms are making the reauthorization process very difficult.

To begin with, there are those who do not accept the main method being used to pressure schools into achieving the overall objectives. The law uses a measurement tool called AYP (adequate yearly progress). Critics of this measurement system have described it as "too inflexible, too arbitrary and too punitive." They point out that even though individual students in schools show significant academic progress, if the school does not reach AYP in every subgroup, students might end up transferring to another school. What is being talked about instead is a more "flexible measure of student improvement known as a growth model." This approach would cause schools to measure the improvement made by individual students each year.

With such a system, "success is defined by a certain amount of growth even if the student isn't on grade level."[1]

Developing a different assessment model that is more flexible and positive will undoubtedly be attempted by Congress during the reauthorization process. A number of ideas have already been suggested for its consideration. As the legislators attempt to reach an agreement on a new model of evaluation, they will have to decide whether the current testing system will remain the sole or primary way to judge student learning and school success. While there is no question that test results can be considered the easiest and most objective measurement tool, there are those who believe that states and individual school districts should be given some freedom to devise their own measures. For example, many schools are requiring students to complete a multidiscipline project in order to meet graduation requirements. Others are mandating a community service requirement.

Senator Russ Feingold has introduced a law titled the Student Achievement Act. As one of the ten senators who voted against No Child Left Behind in 2001, he has never been happy with the law. Thus far he has found ten other current members of the Senate to support his proposal, which opens the door to using several ways for judging student achievement. The legislation allows each school to "demonstrate through multiple measures that they are succeeding by using things like learning projects, portfolio-based assessments, assessments designed by the teacher, [and] graduation rates." This idea has the support of the National Education Association.[2]

While Senator Feingold wishes to reduce the emphasis on testing, others, including President Bush, wish to introduce additional tests at the middle school and high school levels. Whatever assessment system is finally agreed upon, a fundamental question that will most likely be debated is whether curriculum and testing should continue to be the responsibility of the state or if we should have national curriculum and tests. The great discrepancies mentioned earlier between student scores on state and national exam results have caused many to conclude that a nationwide system is the only way we can ensure equal standards between states. *Time* magazine has reported that "the average gap between state and national fourth-grade reading scores is 40 points." The most dramatic difference can be seen by comparing the results in Mississippi, which show that on the state test its students had the highest success rate in the country. On the National Assessment of Educational Progress examination, which is given to students in every state, Mississippi drops to fiftieth place.[3]

As mentioned earlier, former Republican secretaries of education Rod Paige and William Bennett have already supported national examinations. In his new book, *The American Story*, former Democratic Senator Bill Bradley has come to the same conclusion. He recommends "the establishment of national standards for testing and curriculum, especially in math, science, reading and foreign language."[4]

At least during the current discussions over reauthorization, the historic commitment to state and local control of education might well stall any serious effort to establish national curriculums and tests. When such an initiative was considered during the Clinton administration, it ran into a number of problems, especially in trying to create a national social studies or history curriculum. Reaching agreement on what needs to be taught in every subject at every grade level is extremely time consuming. It requires the participation of experts in the field, school administrators as well as practicing teachers. Once the course of study is agreed upon in any curriculum area, developing tests would also be a major challenge. Still, it is possible that during this round of reauthorization debates, steps could be taken to move the United States toward a national system. This is especially true because the public appears ready to consider such an option.

Whether we have state or national examinations, the concern that our schools are too focused on "teaching to the test" is an issue that will face those seeking to rewrite the bill. Both teachers and parents are concerned about this issue. Those in the field of education who consider themselves progressives have already joined the chorus of those upset with the overreliance on tests in targeted curriculum areas. Progressives, who believe students learn best when they are actively involved in their lessons, feel that the heavy emphasis on test results forces teachers to eliminate such useful activities as projects, group learning, and field trips. For them, the pressure of the test is forcing instructors to spend far too much time using traditional teaching methods and focusing on test-taking skills. To those who share this point of view, the reliance on teacher-centered traditional instruction will not help our students to become creative problem solvers.

Many others have pointed out that the mandatory examinations in grades three through eight in language arts and math have caused schools to reduce the time spent in important subjects such as social studies, foreign language, physical education, and health education. As noted earlier, this concern is supported by a number of studies that have been conducted throughout the country. It is possible that to solve this problem, the government could require states to create additional mandatory tests in those curriculum areas that are now not being tested. Another solution is to require schools to increase overall instruction time.

Because school employees would undoubtedly seek additional compensation for spending more time on the job, it is possible that new federal aid to increase salaries could be tied to additional instruction time. Even if new money were available to raise salaries, reaching an agreement on longer school days or an increase in the number of days schools are in session would be difficult. For most school districts, the workday and work year are part of employment contracts negotiated within the district.

On the other hand, it is true that among elected officials, including the current candidates for president, there is support for increasing the compensation for teachers. Most of the politicians and business leaders wish to use additional money for salaries to reward outstanding teaching. Historically in education, such plans have been labeled "merit pay." As mentioned earlier, the idea has seldom been well received by teachers' unions, who frequently have mistrusted any system devised to justify bonuses to the best instructors.

The most likely approach is to have a teacher's effectiveness judged in large part by classroom observations made by principals or other administrators. In most schools, these classroom visits are infrequent, and often at the upper levels, the administrators have limited knowledge of the subject area. For instance, principals often visit a foreign language class even when they do not understand the language being spoken. Teachers also worry about any evaluation system that relies on the judgment of their peers or students. With peers, they worry about how the environment in a school might become more competitive and less civil if teachers were required to judge each other. Most teachers are unanimous in their opposition to any system that relies on student test results as the primary way to evaluate their work. The issue of finding a way to reward the best teachers is a sensitive area that will be considered in the months ahead.

Like pay-for-performance, another issue that appears to have widespread support among political leaders is the expansion of federal support for preschool education programs. It was the federal government that introduced the Head Start Program in 1965. Head Start was designed to allow poor children to experience a free preschool education. With the additional evidence of the positive value of such programs, it is likely that there will be attempts made to increase the availability of this option for many more children. It is possible that such opportunities could be offered by groups other than public schools, and this could include religious agencies.

This opens another difficult issue for Congress, as it considers whether it wishes to expand on the choice options currently included in No Child Left Behind. It is possible to increase the opportunities for faith-based organizations to provide tutoring to students who are failing to meet the required academic standards. One senses that a Democratic Congress and president might be less likely to add money for programs offered by religious groups. On the other hand, Republicans, including President Bush, will advocate for voucher programs that involve allowing students to use their vouchers to attend religious schools.

Choice options could also be expanded between public schools. It has been suggested that a clause be added that would enable students in low-performing schools to transfer outside their home district. Allowing and actually financing such transfers would make it possible for children from urban and rural districts to seek a place in a more effective suburban district. This is one way to deal with schools that are failing, but others look to helping districts.

One of the ways of assisting such schools would be to lower class size. Education Action, a lobbying group for public schools, notes in one of its publications that "if members of Congress question whether class-size really counts, they need only look into the classrooms of schools in which their own kids are enrolled."[5] Needless to say, giving special assistance to low-functioning schools to lower class size would be very costly.

Finances would also be involved in a proposal to expand the charter school movement. This form of choice has had the support not only of Republicans, but also of some Democrats. It is undoubtedly a growing trend at the state level and there will be pressure to provide additional help for the formation of charter schools.

Another issue that will be part of the debate is the goal of providing "highly qualified" teachers in every classroom. Most of the states have made progress in meeting the qualification mandates of the law. The biggest problems in meeting the requirement are being experienced in urban and some very rural school districts. There will also be support for including additional funds for in-service professional training for teachers and administrators. It is possible that such opportunities could be focused in districts and in schools that are having difficulty in recruiting and retaining qualified instructors.

The pressure to do more in almost every area covered in the law, as well as to add such initiatives as improving high schools, will place demands on Congress to consider giving a higher priority to federal aid to education. Most Americans are unaware that the federal government provides less than 10 percent of the money used to finance schools. This being the case, the most important single question facing Congress and the president is how much money they are willing to commit to education. Paying for our current defense costs, as well as what seems to be a questionable and unsteady economy, could even result in reductions in domestic spending, including aid to schools.

At least early in the presidential campaign, there have not been serious discussions about dramatically increasing the nation's overall contribution to financing education. On the other hand, there are those who think it could happen. George Miller, chairman of the House Education and Labor Committee, has written about a "growing consensus that there is a need for greater and sustained investments" in our schools.[6]

Although the issue of the level of federal aid to support education will always be central to almost every aspect of the law, there are parts of the legislation where there seems to be significant agreement. The goal of ensuring safe and drug-free schools is one that is embraced by almost everyone. The same is true with the desire to increase parental involvement in the education process. The business community is especially strong in its advocacy for additional support to expand the technology component of the law. While there seems to be some positive movement in all of these areas, new and improved ways to meet these objectives need to be considered.

Less agreement exists concerning what specific programs should be emphasized in meeting the academic goals of No Child Left Behind. This is especially true in the area of language arts. The administration has strongly supported the Reading First Plan, which has been heavily criticized, especially by leading Democrats. Between 2005 and 2007, there have been several investigations and congressional hearings that have been critical of the administration of Reading First. The inspector general of the Education Department has suggested that "federal officials and consultants had overstepped their authority in steering states to adopt certain curricula and assessments for use in the program, and that there were conflicts of interest among federal decisionmakers who had ties to commercial products purchased by Reading First schools." While the data showed that the program may be helpful, Congress is considering a 60 percent cut in it for the fiscal year that began on 1 October 2007.[7]

There is also a provision in the current law that any academic program that is financed with federal aid must be scientifically verifiable. Educational research is an area that has often been highly controversial. It is possible for studies on an educational program to vary in their conclusions about the effectiveness of any technique or approach. Therefore it is sometimes difficult to prove that what a school district or state is doing is scientifically reliable. Conflicts over the effectiveness of various programs raise the more fundamental question of who should decide how students should be taught. Many in Congress will continue to fight for additional flexibility for state and local districts, while others have less faith in this approach.

Those who believe that there needs to be more flexibility in the law argue that No Child Left Behind is currently too punitive. At the same time, the legislation has also been criticized as being "toothless." Under No Child Left Behind, if a school or district, after several steps of remediation, continues to be unsuccessful, it is required to face radical reconstruction or state takeover. As of January 2008, 1,596 districts had been cited at one level or another as having schools in need of improvement. Of all those, only the state of Maryland had rejected district reform plans and is currently seeking to seize control of its districts' struggling schools. The reaction in many districts that have been named as being unsuccessful is that they need "support not sanctions."[8]

In any case, it is primarily the responsibility of state government to enforce many of the mandates contained in No Child Left Behind. The law establishes "overarching goals and regulations for districts," but the federal Department of Education has left enforcement primarily to the states. In the future, if the federal government concludes that state education departments are avoiding their responsibilities, the federal Department of Education might well become more aggressive in denying funding to schools not meeting the mandates.[9] Like the question of how best to deal with assessment, the issue of federal oversight might need to be reconsidered.

Primarily because of such governance and financial issues, one can understand why the reauthorization debate is likely not to be settled prior to the 2008 elections. With a new president and changes in Congress, it is not unreasonable to predict that even in 2009, the law will not be reauthorized. Because of the provision that the current legislation will stay in effect, there is not a deadline that must be met. Given this situation, we can only guess at the likely future of this landmark legislation. The purpose of the final chapter is to consider the possibilities.

NOTES

1. Claudia Wallis and Sonja Steptoe, "How to Fix No Child Left Behind," *Time*, 24 May 2007, www.time.com/time/printout/0,8816,1625192,00.htm.

2. Russ Feingold, "Q & A," *NEA Today*, January 2008, 19.

3. Wallis and Steptoe, "How to Fix No Child Left Behind."

4. Bill Bradley, *The New American Story* (New York: Random House, 2007), 171.

5. Education Action, "Break Your Silence on NCLB," Cambridge Institute for Public Education, ed-action.org/states.php?section=NCLB (accessed 6 December 2007).

6. U.S. Rep. George Miller, "Chairman Miller Remarks on the Future of the No Child Left Behind Education Law," 30 July 2007, speech at the National Press Club, www.house.gov/apps/list/speech/edlabor_dem/RelJul30N CLBSpeech.html.

7. Kathleen Kennedy Manzo, "Massive Funding Cuts to 'Reading First' Generate Worries for Struggling Schools," *Education Week*, 14 January 2008, www.edweek.org/ew/articles/2008/01/16/19read.h27.html.

8. Joe Williams, "District Accountability: More Bark Than Bite?" *Scholastic*, January 2008, content.scholastic.com/browse/article.jsp?id=3748578 (accessed 11 January 2008).

9. Williams, "District Accountability."

15

WHAT IS AHEAD?

The first question that must be addressed concerning the future of No Child Left Behind is whether or not there will be some sort of reauthorization bill passed during the next three years. Congress could follow the advice of former Democratic presidential candidate Bill Richardson and "scrap" the law totally. For several reasons, such an outcome appears to be unlikely. To begin with, Congress must act on reauthorization or, according to the original wording in the law, it will stay in effect as it is indefinitely. There is enough dissatisfaction with many aspects of No Child Left Behind that it would seem improbable that Congress would allow letting it continue as it is now written.

Given the fact that the federal government has passed major legislation to assist schools for more than forty years, it is inconceivable that our elected officials would totally abolish programs that have become so important to the financial support of education in the United States. While there is a small core of conservatives in Congress who would prefer to return all or most of the responsibility for schools to the state and local governments, the number of such lawmakers is quite small. Even with our growing national deficit and the prospect of a recession, Congress and whoever becomes president are very unlikely to totally abandon the nation's schools.

On the other hand, the size of the future financial commitment of the federal government to education is very much in question. As the 2008 presidential campaign continues, it appears that education is not even among the top five issues on the minds of the voters. Candidates are talking much more about the economy, the war in Iraq, the overall threat of terrorism, immigration, the environment, and even social issues such as race, gender, and abortion. Still, No Child Left Behind is an issue that must be faced. When serious consideration is finally given to the law, there are a number of dilemmas facing our leaders.

Chairman George Miller of the House Education and Labor Committee has even questioned whether the name of the law might have to be changed. He suggested that the title is currently too closely linked to a very unpopular president. This is a minor concern compared to some of the other questions that must be resolved. Following the *Nation at Risk* report in 1983, our country gradually developed a three-pronged approach to improving schools. The first step was to articulate what educators have labeled "curriculum standards." These standards can be defined as what students should know and be able to do in every area of the school curriculum. The first major determination that had to be made during the early days of the standards movement was whether we should have national or state curriculum standards.

In 2001, the Republican Party, which controlled the Congress, along with President Bush, favored state control of curriculum and testing. As we have seen, a number of prominent individuals and groups have concluded that it is now time to again consider a national curriculum. As noted earlier, support for this approach can also be found in public opinion surveys. Even the national media are writing about the need to move in this direction. In a cover article published in *U.S. News & World Report*, the author quotes one critic of the current system as claiming that it is causing a "race to the bottom."[1] Certainly the great discrepancies between state and national test results point to a problem with the present system.

A change to national curriculum standards would not be an easy process that could take place quickly. The lack of support for such a dramatic step at the state level and apparently by a majority of teachers and administrators will slow any movement in this direction. At the same time, as noted earlier, it is possible that during the reauthorization process, the first steps might be taken to make national standards a reality in the future.

After the development of state curriculum standards, the second initiative was to create an assessment plan to determine if students were meeting the prescribed educational objectives. The result, in large part because of the mandates of No Child Left Behind, was a system of evaluating students and schools based on what has been labeled "high-stakes testing." It is these tests, created at the state level, that have caused a major backlash against the law. There are charges that teachers are being forced to "teach to the test" and that other areas of the curriculum that are not evaluated by mandated tests are being neglected. It has also been shown that many states have created very low academic expectations for their students.

More recently, critics of state testing have concluded that what is needed is neither state nor national tests. These individuals point to the need of our country to compete internationally. As a result, they believe that it is "time to think global in testing U.S. students."[2] For some, it is more important to compare our student test scores with those of other nations than it is to worry about differences between the states. The present assessment plan created by No Child Left Behind will undoubtedly be a major topic considered by Congress in the days ahead.

After the creation of curriculum standards and high-stakes testing, the final strategy that has evolved to improve our schools is called accountability. It has been determined that schools that are not meeting predetermined goals should be subject to certain consequences and remedial measures. As we have seen, No Child Left Behind established a measurement called adequate yearly progress as the way of determining the effectiveness of schools. The approach has not been universally accepted in the field and is undergoing reevaluation. The most popular alternative may be to create a method that attempts to measure individual student progress or growth rather than expecting schools to reach a predetermined goal for all students in a particular classification. There is also support for a change in focus that would provide more help for troubled schools rather than resorting to measures that some critics feel are too punitive.

Proposals such as these are colored somewhat by the political positions represented among our leaders. There are significant differences between the two major parties in specific areas: Many Republicans are more supportive of giving additional authority for managing schools to the state governments and local school districts. While no Democrats would call for a totally nationalized education system, many are more likely to support a more active federal presence in public education. This is seen primarily in the Democratic commitment to provide more equality of educational opportunity, not only between the states but within the states.

Partisan differences may also be seen in the amount of money that members of the two parties are willing to spend on education. The most important attraction of the original No Child Left Behind law for many Democrats was the promise of the Bush administration to allot a significant amount of new aid to education. As a result, a major roadblock to any reauthorization legislation will be the size of the total aid commitment made available by the law.

The issue of funding No Child Left Behind may become even more complicated as a result of a ruling in January 2008. In the case *Pontiac School District v. Spellings*, the U.S. Court of Appeals for the 6th Circuit voted two to one for the plaintiff against the federal government. Based on the following wording in the majority decision, the National Education Association, which originally brought the case to court, is claiming that if the federal government does not provide sufficient funding for the mandates required under No Child Left Behind, individual school districts may choose to ignore the law:

The No Child Left Behind Act rests on the most laudable of goals: to ensure that all children have a fair, equal, and significant opportunity to obtain a high-quality education. Nobody challenges that aim. But a state official deciding to participate in NCLB could reasonably read [the un-funded-mandates provision] to mean that her state need not comply with requirements that are "not paid for under the act" through federal funds.[3]

Speaking for the federal government, Education Secretary Margaret Spellings made it known that "the decision was far from the last word on the subject. No Child Left Behind is strong and on the books, and will be abided by by the states and the federal government."[4] While potentially this decision could create some havoc for efforts to enforce the law, it will undoubtedly be appealed to the Supreme Court. Still, it does place an additional cloud over the reauthorization process.

Another potential area of difference is the question of support for choice options. Leading Republicans, along with President Bush, have consistently favored a voucher system that includes private schools. Unless the control of the federal government somehow becomes dominated by conservative Republicans, adoption of any such program is unlikely. Even though choice programs allowing vouchers to be used in nonpublic schools will most likely not be part of the new law, there remains growing support in many states for charter schools. It is not difficult to conceive a reauthorization bill that gives additional impetus to this trend.

Combining the principle of choice with that of "faith-based initiatives," which is a section included in the original law, could be another contentious issue. This conflict might also be one that will cause a division between the political parties. President Bush and his supporters in Congress will undoubtedly seek to broaden the role played by faith-based organizations. Democrats, who will be pushed by the teacher unions and other public-school groups, are less likely to be willing to spend federal money to assist parochial schools and for services provided by groups other than the public schools.

Even though there are portions of the law where partisan politics might create conflict, there are some areas where consensus will likely prove to be easier. As we have seen earlier, there is a growing concern about the need to improve our high schools. Specifically, many are very worried about the alarming dropout rate in some of our schools. It has been argued that No Child Left Behind does currently appear to focus on the elementary level, with some attention paid to grades seven and eight. The need to give additional assistance to high schools is widely felt.

A second initiative, which is very popular, especially with leading Democrats, is the desire to do more to encourage preschool education. In addition, both parties are likely to agree on continuing to pursue the effort to ensure that there is a "highly qualified" teacher in every classroom. The fact that we seem to have had some success in this effort has been demonstrated in several recent studies. *USA Today* carried a claim that "beginning teachers have better academic credentials than their predecessors did a decade ago, suggesting that tougher requirements at all levels—from the federal government to the local teachers' college—have forced teachers' colleges to improve offerings while luring more qualified candidates into teaching."[5]

A second study in Louisiana concluded that first-year teachers "can match" the test results of veteran instructors.[6] It is likely that Congress will wish to continue the efforts to improve both teachers and paraprofessionals. In order to do so, there will need to be money set aside for ongoing professional training and possibly funds to support improvements in teacher preparation programs.

While the differences over issues vary in intensity, the resolution of the reauthorization debates most likely will depend on the outcome of the 2008 election. It is extremely difficult to imagine a scenario where the president and Congress, in a spirit of bipartisanship, will be able to come together and find a way to pass a reauthorization bill prior to November 2008. Undoubtedly, President Bush would like to find a way to accomplish this task, as such a bill would ensure the continuation of a major part of the legacy of his presidency. He made his feelings clear concerning the importance of reauthorizing No Child Left Behind in his 2008 State of the Union address. Unfortunately, given the federal government's recent history in dealing with controversial issues, a better prediction would be that such legislation might be agreed upon late in 2009 or even 2010. Whenever serious discussions occur, it is easy to agree with a conclusion of David S. Seeley, who wrote in *Education Week* that "the most important challenge facing public education today involves its *systematic reform*, and this need not be a partisan matter."[7]

Many believe that "systematic reform" or fundamental changes in our approach to improving education is what is necessary. According to Jack Jennings and Diane Stark Rentner, writing in *Phi Delta Kappan*, "the key question is whether the strengths of this legislation can be retained while its weaknesses are addressed."[8] Even if the law is greatly improved and additional financial resources are committed to education, schools alone cannot solve the academic problems of our children.

The idea expressed in the African proverb that "it takes the whole village to raise a child" has never been truer than in our country today. When one examines some of the social statistics describing our children and their families, it is easy to see the magnitude of the problems facing our schools. We need to take seriously the implications of the following facts:

- Only two-thirds of American children now live in two-parent homes. (Only 35 percent of non-Hispanic black children live in such homes.)
- The number of unmarried opposite or same-sex partners living together has more than doubled. A significant number of our children are coming from this type of home.
- In 1960, fewer than half of married women with children between the ages of six and seventeen worked outside the home. Currently we have approximately 80 percent of these mothers working outside the home. The change has been even greater for married women with children under six. It has gone from one in five to three in five.
- The number of so-called "latchkey" children has increased dramatically. On average these children are watching television twenty-five hours per week.
- Half of new marriages now end in divorce.
- One in five American children are living in poverty. (This includes 33 percent of black children and 29 percent of Hispanic children.)
- An estimated one million American children experience homelessness over the course of a given year.

- One third of American high-school students drop out of school.
- Twenty percent of high-school students and 10 percent of middle-school students admit to using "illicit drugs."
- During the past twenty-five years, suicides of those between age 15 and 24 have tripled.[9]

In addressing the issues noted above, we need to give consideration to the research that reinforces the importance of parental involvement in the education of their children. No Child Left Behind recognizes this priority, but there is concern that this aspect of the law is not working well. A study completed by the Appleseed Foundation found that "inadequate parental involvement is hindering fulfillment of the federal No Child Left Behind program's goal to improve the nation's schools and produce better students."[10] Simple solutions, such as somehow getting parents to talk more to their children at home, appear to pay educational dividends. It has been suggested in an article titled "The Key to Your Child Doing Well at School? Conversation in the Home" that "children from the poorest homes may do worse at school because parents do not talk to them enough." Such a conclusion came from a study led by the Cambridge-based professor Robin Alexander.[11]

Another educational research agency has recommended a concept called "family literacy." Such an approach has been described as follows:

Family literacy directly affects the role and effectiveness of parents in helping their children learn. If parents understand the language and literacy lessons their children learn in school, they can more easily provide the experiences necessary for their children to succeed. Bringing parents and children together to learn in an educational setting is the core of family literacy and the way to provide parents with firsthand experiences about what their children learn and how they are taught.

The four components of comprehensive family literacy include:

Interactive literacy activities between parents and their children.
Parent training on how to be their child's first and most important teacher and how to participate as a full partner in their child's education.
Literacy training for parents that leads to economic self-sufficiency.

Age-appropriate education for children to prepare them for success in school and life.[12]

An article in the *Buffalo Evening News* talked specifically about the ways that parents can help their children at home. After providing them with the necessary food, shelter, clothing, adequate sleep, and love, parents or guardians must be able to:

- Look around to find real-life education experiences: Extend and expand your child's curiosity.
- Listen and talk with your children about what you see and find together. Conversation and language building are keys to school and life success.
- Provide for sensible routine and structure in your day. When do we read books? How long do we watch TV or use the computer?[13]

The Public Education Network, a major nonprofit organization, has done a three-year study on how parents judged the results of the No Child Left Behind law. After holding public hearings in twenty-five locations throughout the United States, the group published a number of interesting conclusions, including that "NCLB pays considerable lip service to parent involvement; in reality, parents and communities are almost shut out of the reform process." The authors of the study also believe that along with paying too little attention to parents, the law fails to adequately involve local communities. The final report of the group goes on to point out that the authors believe that there is one single overwhelming flaw in the legislation. For these researchers, "NCLB has been imposed on a public school system that remains unequal."[14]

Charges that our system of financing public education fails to provide equal opportunity for all children did not begin with the criticism of No Child Left Behind. Jonathan Kozol and others have been writing about this issue for decades. Simply visiting schools in affluent suburbs and comparing them with those in most urban and rural districts will quickly convince even the casual observer of the dramatic differences. The discrepancies show up not only when one compares the actual buildings and grounds of the school, but also the contrasting class sizes and availability of supplies and technology. Careful study of the salaries and the training, as well as the experience, of the faculty also demonstrates the differences. These discrepancies result in large part because of the way we finance public-school education in this country. Over 40 percent of the money used to pay for public schools is raised by property taxes.

Districts with a large tax base, whether it is the result of expensive homes, industrial complexes, or shopping malls located in the community, are able to more easily raise money from property taxes. As a result, these "rich" districts can often spend two or three times as much on a student's education as a property-poor district. Add to this the fact that the poorer schools almost always have more educational challenges than affluent schools. Urban and some rural districts often have more non-English speaking children, as well as more students needing expensive special education programs. The additional cost of educating these children only adds to the financial challenges faced by poor districts. Because of conditions at home, five-year-olds from the less affluent communities often enter kindergarten much less well prepared than children in suburban schools. This too increases the responsibilities of these schools.

It has become the role of state governments, and to a lesser degree, the federal government, to somehow give extra aid to communities with low property wealth. Unfortunately in most states, the aid formulas have not come close to creating equal educational opportunities for all children. To remedy this situation, many poor districts have instituted lawsuits to force the state legislatures to at least provide adequate financial aid to allow the schools to offer a quality education for all students. In several states, these cases have brought about some improvement, but thus far they are falling short of solving the problem of inequality. This has occurred in part because governors and state legislatures have chosen to challenge or ignore court decisions that attempt to set parameters on what they feel is their prerogative to establish aid formulas. Whether it is done at the state level or by the federal government, we will not solve our education problems until we face up to the fact that this country is not providing equal educational opportunities, especially for our poor children. A letter to the editor in a local paper written by a retired teacher in Rochester, New York, expresses his strongly felt views about this issue. He writes: "It is not the schools! So what is it? . . . 88 percent of Rochester students live in poverty. . . . It's not the teachers, the curriculum, the building, or the programs. It's the families and their poverty. . . . But constantly blaming the school district is useless political rhetoric. Until change comes to the community, no significant improvement will come to the city schools' performance."[15]

On a more hopeful note, an article in *Education Week* suggests that "reasons exist to believe that the federal No Child Left Behind Act could shrink the 'poverty gap' that finds students from poor families trailing behind their better-off peers in school." The author balances this bit of optimism by noting that the law could also have a negative effect. She worries about the fact that failing schools could lose financial aid "as families take advantage of the tutoring or school choice options that the law provides."[16]

There is little doubt that poverty in the United States remains a serious problem and that it affects the children attending our schools. Middle-class Americans, in recent decades, have also been experiencing increasing difficulty in supporting their families. Because so many parents from the middle class have moved into the workforce and the number of single-parent families has grown, it has become more difficult for these individuals to remain actively engaged in the education of their children. In his recent book *The Conscience of a Liberal*, economist Paul Krugman highlighted how those in the highest income levels have dramatically increased their share of the national income. Since 1980, the overall "median family income has risen only 0.7 percent a year." Wages of those on the lower rungs of the income scale, including those receiving the national minimum wage, have dramatically lost purchasing power during the same period.[17] In 2005, the richest 10 percent of Americans received 44.3 percent of the national income, while the top one percent gained 17.4 percent.[18]

Similar economic conditions, where the rich controlled a high percentage of the income, were also present in the 1920s. The Depression and World War II created in America a "middle class society." In a section of the book that Krugman calls "the new economics of inequality," he points to the dramatically lower tax rates on the rich, reduced capital gains taxes, and reduced inheritance taxes, along with other policies since the mid-1980s that have resulted in greater economic inequality.

At the same time, there has been a decline in the percentage of American workers represented by unions, brought about, at least in part, by unfriendly government policies and actions. This trend has reduced the ability of many middle-class employees to bargain for higher wages and better fringe benefits. Does family income matter in education? Krugman and other observers think it does. He agrees that there is a "highly uneven quality of U.S. basic education." For him, "what it all comes down to is that although the principle of 'equality of opportunity, not equality of results' sounds fine, it's a largely fictitious distinction."[19]

During the mid-1960s, President Lyndon Johnson began what he called the War on Poverty. A significant element of this initiative was the passage of the 1965 law known as the Elementary Secondary Education Act. This legislation was the first major thrust of the federal government into the field of education. Of course it was this law that, in 2001, was renamed the No Child Left Behind act. It should be remembered that this legislation was only one aspect of the national goal to eliminate poverty and allow all Americans an equal chance at pursuing the American dream.

The Vietnam War and the fact that those presidential administrations immediately after President Johnson were less than enthusiastic about antipoverty programs caused Johnson's War on Poverty to have only a limited effect. In this first decade of the twenty-first century, our nation again faces many challenges, including the distribution of national income and a seemingly beleaguered middle class. These issues are directly related to the problems facing our schools. Still, if we as a nation are to be serious about leaving no child behind, our country must look to find ways to reduce the effects of poverty and improve family stability. This cannot be done by laws alone. Communities, private charities, and religious organizations must all do their part.

At the same time, the debate over the reauthorization of No Child Left Behind is significant in that it will allow our government to again consider what can be done to improve the education of our children. The importance of this endeavor was highlighted by Abraham Lincoln when he gave his first public speech in Illinois in 1834. The young candidate said, "Upon the subject of education, not presuming to dictate any plan or system respecting it, I can only say that I view it as the most important subject which we as a people can be engaged in."[20] If we accept Lincoln's priority as a nation, there is little question that we can come much closer to ensuring that no child is left behind.

NOTES

1. Eddy Ramirez, "Room to Improve," *U.S. News & World Report*, 12 November 2007, 50.

2. Raymond C. Scheppach, "Time to Think Global in Testing U.S. Students," Stateline.org, 19 November 2007, www.stateline.org/live/details/story?contentId=258849.

3. Mark Walsh, "Judges' View of Federal Law," *Education Week*, 16 January 2008, 19.

4. Walsh, "Judges' View of Federal Law," 1.

5. Greg Toppo, "Teacher Qualifications Improve in the Past Decade," *USA Today*, 13 December 2007, www.usatoday.com/news/education/2007-12-11-teacher-qualifications_N.htm.

6. Vaishali Honawar, "Gains Seen in Retooled Teacher Ed," *Education Week*, 31 October 2007, 1.

7. David S. Seeley, "Where Is Education in the 2008 Election?" *Education Week*, 9 January 2008, 40.

8. Jack Jennings and Diane Stark Rentner, "Ten Big Effects of the No Child Left Behind Act on Public Schools," *Phi Delta Kappan*, October 2006, 113.

9. David Miller Sadker, Myra Pollack Sadker, and Karen R. Zittleman, *Teachers, Schools, and Society* (Boston: McGraw-Hill, 2007), 191–200.

10. Kent Allen, "Parent Involvement in NCLB School Standards Is Found Lacking," *U.S. News & World Report*, 27 September 2006, www.usnews.com/usnews/news/articles/060927/27nclb.htm.

11. Richard Garner, "The Key to Your Child Doing Well at School? Conversation in the Home," *The Independent*, 14 December 2007, news.independent.co.uk/education/education_news/article3249890.ece.

12. Theresa Clarke, *Family Literacy: A Strategy for Educational Improvement*, NGA Center for Best Practices, 8 November 2002, www.nga.org/Files/pdf/110802LITERACY.pdf.

13. Dorothy Rich, "It's Time to Focus on Family's Role in Educating Children," *Buffalo Evening News*, 30 December 2007.

14. Public Education Network, *Open to the Public: How Communities, Parents, and Students Assess the Impact of the No Child Left Behind Act: 2004–2007, The Realities Left Behind*, July 2007, www.publiceducation .org/nclb_main/2007_NCLB_National_Report.pdf.

15. David Reilly, "Helping the Schools," *City*, 14–20 November 2007, 4.

16. Debra Viadero, "No Easy Answers About NCLB's Effect on 'Poverty Gap,'" *Education Week*, 8 November 2007, www.edweek.org/ew/articles/ 2007/11/14/12brookings.h27.html.

17. Paul Krugman, *The Conscience of a Liberal* (New York: W. W. Norton, 2007), 55.

18. Krugman, *The Conscience of a Liberal*, 16.

19. Krugman, *The Conscience of a Liberal*, 249.

20. "Abraham Lincoln Quotes and Quotations," www.topicscites.com/ abraham-lincoln/quotes.htm (accessed 7 April 2004).

INDEX

ABOUT THE AUTHOR

William Hayes has been a high-school social studies teacher, depart-ment chair, assistant principal, and high-school principal. From 1973 to 1994, he served as superintendent of schools for the Byron-Bergen Central School District, which is located eighteen miles west of Rochester, New York. During his career, he was an active member of the New York State Council of Superintendents, and he is the author of a council publication titled *The Superintendency: Thoughts for New Superintendents*, which is used to prepare new superintendents in New York state.

He has also written a number of articles for various educational journals. After retiring from the superintendency, he served as chair of the Teacher Education Division at Roberts Wesleyan Col-lege in Rochester until 2003. He currently remains a full-time teacher at Roberts Wesleyan. During the past nine years, he has written eleven books, which have all been published by Scarecrow Education Press and Rowman & Littlefield Education. They are *Real-Life Case Studies for School Administrators*, *Real-Life Case Studies for Teachers*, *So You Want to Be a Superintendent?*, *So You Want to Be a School Board Member?*, *Real-Life Case Studies for*

School Board Members, So You Want to Become a College Professor?, So You Want to Become a Principal?, Are We Still a Nation at Risk Two Decades Later?, Horace Mann's Vision of the Public Schools: Is It Still Relevant?, The Progressive Education Movement: Is It Still a Factor in Today's Schools?, and *All New Real-Life Case Studies for Administrators*.